NANCY'S CANDY COOKBOOK

How To Make Candy at Home
the Easy Way

Nancy Shipman

Rayve Productions Inc.
Windsor, California

Published by   **Rayve Productions Inc.**
                      POB 726 Windsor CA 95492 USA

Printed in the United States of America

Publisher's Cataloging in Publication

Shipman, Nancy
  Nancy's candy cookbook : how to make candy at home the easy way
/ by Nancy Shipman
  p. cm.
  Includes index.
  ISBN 1-877810-65-7

  1. Candy. I. Title.

TX791.S55 1996   641.8'53

Library of Congress Catalog Card Number 95-68633

Illustrations by Randall F. Ray

Cover photo courtesy of Hershey's Chocolate Co.

I dedicate this book to . . .

❧ My wonderful mom, who taught me the joys of cooking at a very early age.

My sincerest thanks to . . .

❦ My sweet husband for his encouragement and support.

❦ Bob and Virginia Hoffman for their professional guidance and editing of my recipes.

❦ The great staff at Nancy's Fancy's Inc. for sampling all my recipes.

CONTENTS

Introduction 7
    Equipment & Supplies 9
    Candy-making Ingredients 10
    Tips for Candy-making Success 14
    Chocolate, The Most Important Ingredient 15
    How to Temper Real Chocolate 16
    Summer Coating — How To Melt and Use It 17
    Dipping and Coating 18
    Candy Molds Care and Use 19
    How to Make Candy in Molds 20
    Candy Painting 25

Fudge 27

Brittles & Barks 55

Caramels and Nougats 65

Nuts, Clusters and Chews 79

Cream Centers 93

Fruit and Nut Centers 109

Mints and Jellies 121

Childhood Fantasies 131

Holiday Treats 143

Truffles 163

Nancy Shipman's Story 181

Nancy's Classes on Videotape 182

Nancy's Fancy's Store Supplies 183

Index 185

INTRODUCTION

Candy-making Is Easy and Fun

Quality candies are the sweetest part of life — tasty treats we appreciate and savor from our first childhood candy cane to those wonderfully rich, grown-up truffles. As a professional who teaches candy-making, I have found that most people are surprised to discover how easy it is to make top-quality candies. Not only is candy-making easy, it is also great fun!

I invite you to join me in candy-making adventures. In no time at all you'll be turning out impressive and delicious candies perfect for serving or giving as gifts — Grandma's traditional fudge and taffy, divinity, pralines, peppermint patties, fruit and nut eggs, truffles, divinity, candied violets and myriad other sweet fantasies.

Sweets to the sweet!

Equipment and Supplies

Most of the things you need to make candy are already in your cupboards. Additional specialized cooking items are inexpensive and easily found in candy-making supply stores or by mail from the author's store (see pages 183-184).

• **A stove**, gas or electric, or even a hot plate with temperature controls.

• **Pots and pans**. A double boiler with a lid, and 1½, 3, and 4 quart heavy saucepans with lids. Aluminum and cast iron are fine. You'll need an 8-inch square pan, a 9 x 13-inch pan, and a cookie sheet, as well. Two mixing bowls, one small and one medium, should be adequate.

• **Utensils**. A couple of wooden cooking spoons, and a couple of rubber spatulas, one large and one small. Some knives for chopping, cutting and slicing.

• **Measuring utensils**. Two measuring cups, one for liquid and one for dry ingredients, and a set of measuring spoons. A kitchen scale will be helpful, but is not essential. One or two medicine droppers. (The ones that come with eye drops are fine, just wash and dry thoroughly).

• **A candy thermometer**. This is really important. It should measure from 30 to 300 degrees Fahrenheit, have a metal clip to hold it on the side of a pot, and have numbers large enough for you to read easily. Don't stint on this. Get a good one!

• **Parchment paper and plastic wrap**.

• **A table model mixer**, with several different speeds for mixing and blending.

• **A rolling pin**, preferably of marble, but wood will do.

• **A marble slab**, 16 x 20 inches is an ideal surface for making candy, particularly when you are making cooked candy, nougats or brittle. Marble does not absorb or retain heat and it stays cool, making it very easy to form candies on. (**Note:** Don't use your marble slab as a cutting board or hot pad. It scratches easily and scratches will ruin the smooth surface you need for candy making).

• **Specialty items**. To make some candies, you will need special molds, dipping spoons, colorings, flavorings, oils, etc. If you can't find these items locally, you can order them through Nancy Shipman's store (see pages 183-184).

Candy-making Ingredients

The candy-making products listed below can be purchased at candy-making and cake-decorating stores unless otherwise indicated. To order directly from Nancy Shipman's store, see pages 183-184.

Acetic acid: A strong vinegar concentrate that can be obtained from a pharmacist, used to reduce sweetness in candy.

Almond paste: A smooth, heavy dough made of ground almonds, often used in candies and pastries.

Baking soda: Sodium bicarbonate. Used in some candy recipes, especially brittles, to produce a honeycomb texture.

Brown sugar: Granulated sugar with molasses added. Light brown sugar is milder in flavor and is generally preferred in candy making.

Candy coloring: Powdered food coloring or oil-based food coloring. This is very concentrated and does not change the consistency of candy of fillings. **Note:** Food coloring found in grocery stores has a water base and should not be used in candy making.

Caster sugar: Also called "super-fine granulated sugar," often used to make candy centers because it dissolves and incorporates faster than standard granulated sugar.

Chocolate: A preparation of the seeds of cacao, often sweetened and flavored. Real milk, white or dark chocolate requires tempering prior to candy making in order to set up properly. (See *How to Temper Real Chocolate*, page 16)

Citric acid: A colorless, translucent acid, available in liquid or crystal powder form. Citric acid improves candy quality and flavor, especially in fruit candies.

Coconut oil: One of the ingredients in summer coating. Used to thin and soften chocolate and decrease brittleness.

Confectioners' coating: Also called "summer coating" or "summer chocolate."

Confectioners' ginger: Also called "candied ginger."

Confectioners' sugar: Also called "powdered sugar." This is very fine sugar with cornstarch added. Always sift before measuring. **Note:** Do not substitute confectioners' sugar for granulated or brown sugar.

Corn syrup: Light-weight, clear-colored syrup used in most candy recipes to prevent graininess. **Note:** Do not substitute dark corn syrup for light.

Cream: For most recipes, use heavy cream (whipping cream) unless otherwise called for.

Desiccated (macaroon) coconut: Finely cut, dry unsweetened coconut used for coconut centers.

Drivert sugar: Fondant sugar with invertase in it used for creamier centers and to make the clear center in chocolate covered cherries.

Dry corn syrup: Powdered corn syrup. When using in recipes, do not reconstitute unless recipe indicates otherwise. To substitute for liquid corn syrup, add 5 parts corn syrup powder to 1 part water, by weight. Heat over low heat until dissolved.

Dry egg white: Also called "egg albumen." To reconstitute, add 1 tablespoon of powder to 2 tablespoons of water and mix well. Use 2 tablespoons of reconstituted egg white for each egg in recipe.

Dry fondant: A commercial powdered sugar product that is finer than powdered sugar obtained in grocery stores.

Frappé: Also called "marshmallow cream."

Glucose: Concentrated corn syrup, often used in cream centers. It makes cooked candies firmer.

Honey: Natural bee honey in liquid form can be used in any recipe calling for honey. A variety of flavors are available. **Note:** Do not use creamed honey or honey spreads.

Invert sugar: Liquid sugar. It improves candy's quality and keeping properties. If invert sugar crystallizes, place it over hot water to liquify.

Invertase: A yeast derivative, used in fondant centers for creamier texture. Invertase can be omitted from any recipe.

Lecithin: An emulsifier made from soybeans and used to keep oils from separating in candies such as caramels.

Molasses: A thick syrup produced in refining raw sugar, ranging from light to dark brown in color. Any type may be used in candy recipes specifying molasses.

Non-dairy liquid coffee creamer: Available in frozen and liquid form. May be used as a substitute for whipping cream in fudge recipes.

Nulomoline: Also called "invert sugar."

Oils and flavorings: Oils or very concentrated flavorings are ideal for candy making. Their flavors are stronger so very little is necessary, and they do not thin candy or fillings. Flavorings that are water based may harden chocolate.

Paramount crystals: Vegetable oils, mostly coconut oil, sold in small shaved pieces, and used to thin chocolate.

Raw chip coconut: Unsweetened wide coconut sold in health food stores. It is an excellent addition to brittle.

Royal icing/frosting: Decorator's frosting made with powdered sugar, water and meringue powder, used to make specialty decorations on candies, cakes and panorama eggs. This icing dries very hard.

Sugar: Granulated cane sugar.

Summer coating/summer chocolate: Commercially produced chocolate and colored candy made with coconut or vegetable oils, not cocoa butter. It does not require tempering to set up as real chocolate does. It is easy to use — simply melt over hot tap water — and is available in a variety of delicious flavors and colors that make quality candies.

Tips for Candy-making Success

1. **Always check your thermometer before making candy.** It is very important to check your thermometer for accuracy each time you use it. To check for accuracy, place the thermometer in a pan of water and bring the water to a boil. Let it boil for 3 to 4 minutes. The thermometer should read 212 degrees. Your thermometer must be accurate for candy-making success.

2. **Read the entire recipe before you begin making candy.**

3. **Be sure you have all the ingredients for your recipe before you begin.**

4. **Measure all ingredients before you begin.**

5. **If you are using real chocolate of any kind, it must be tempered to set up correctly** (see *How to Temper Real Chocolate*, page 16).

6. **Always melt summer coating over hot tap water** (see *Summer Coating*, page 17). **Do not** try to melt summer coating on the stove; it is too hot for summer coating.

Chocolate
The Most Important Ingredient

As chocolate is the most important ingredient, it should, obviously, be given special attention as to the kind you buy, how you store it, and how you use it.

Baking Chocolate is the purest form of chocolate. It is very bitter, and in this stage, it is hard to imagine that it can become delicious candy!

Milk Chocolate is the chocolate "liquor" that has extra cocoa butter, milk or cream, sugar, and vanilla added.

Sweet Chocolate and Semi-Sweet Chocolate are processed in the same manner as milk chocolate, but milk solids are not included.

White Chocolate, according the Food and Drug Administration, is not chocolate, because the cocoa liquor has been removed in processing. It is usually labeled as "Confectioners' Coating."

Dietetic Chocolate is Sweet- or Semi-Sweet Chocolate that is made with an artificial sweetener instead of sugar. Note: It is made for persons on sugar-restricted diets. It is not for weight-loss diets. It has more calories than most other chocolates.

All of these types of chocolate must be "tempered" before you can use them to make candy.

Tempering chocolate is easy to do, takes very little time, but must be done properly to give your finished candies the look and taste of candies made by a professional candy maker.

Tempering simply means that you raise and lower the temperature of the chocolate. This prevents that unappetizing grayish color, or "bloom," on chocolate candy and allows the chocolate to set up again after melting.

How to Temper Real Chocolate

Real chocolate must be "tempered" before you use it for molding or dipping. In fillings or fudge, tempering is not necessary. Tempering chocolate is easy to do, but must be done properly to give your finished candies the look and taste of candies made by a professional candy maker.

Simply put, tempering is the process of raising and lowering the chocolate's temperature. This prevents that unappetizing grayish color, or "bloom," on chocolate candy, and allows the chocolate to set up firmly again after melting.

1. Chop or grate a half pound of chocolate. (Use larger quantities after you've had some practice). The smaller the pieces, the faster it will melt.

2. Fill the lower pan of a double boiler with hot water at about 140 degrees.

3. Put the chocolate pieces in the top pan of the double boiler and place on top of lower pan.

4. Fasten your candy thermometer* on the side of the top pan, not permitting the bottom of the thermometer to rest on the bottom of the pan.

5. Stir the melting chocolate frequently with a wooden spoon or rubber spatula, keeping an eye on the temperature.

6. When the thermometer reaches 112 degrees, remove top pan from bottom, and replace hot water with cold tap water. Stirring constantly, lower the temperature of the milk chocolate until it is thick like frosting.

7. Replace the cold water in the bottom pan with hot water, about 140 degrees, and while stirring constantly, raise the temperature of the chocolate to 85 degrees for milk or white chocolate, and 88 degrees for dark chocolate. **Warning:** If you heat the chocolate hotter than the temperatures indicated, you have to start all over.

Test the accuracy of your thermometer by placing it in a pan of hot water. Bring the water to a boil, and boil 3 to 4 minutes. The thermometer should read 212 degrees at sea level, and 1 degree less for every 500 feet above sea level. If yours doesn't, simply add or subtract the number of degrees required.

Summer Coating —
How To Melt and Use It

Summer coating is a delicious and easy-to-use candy-making ingredient. It is commercially produced chocolate and colored candy made with coconut or vegetable oils, not cocoa butter; and it does not need to be tempered. Summer coating is usually sold in round-bottomed shapes, although some brands are a ribbon or rectangular shape. Melt summer coatings as follows:

1. Clean and dry candy molds.

2. Place summer coating in top of double boiler.

3. Melt summer coating over hot tap water. DO NOT COOK ON THE STOVE. If overheated, coating will thicken and get lumpy. Often it can be cooled and remelted, but it's better to simply avoid overheating.

4. Electric skillet or warming tray, even a heating pad, can be used to melt summer coating. Let the surface heat up on the lowest temperature and check it by placing your hand on the surface. If the surface is too hot for your hand, it is too hot for the candy. Turn the temperature down and/or place a folded towel on the surface before putting the container of candy on the surface.

Your microwave can also be used to melt summer coating. But be careful, candy can burn very quickly. Set your microwave on High, then check and stir every 20-30 seconds to see if candy is melted.

5. DO NOT MIX WATER INTO SUMMER COATING*

6. DO NOT MIX LIQUEUR INTO SUMMER COATING*

7. Stir to hasten melting.

*Water and liqueur cannot be used to thin or flavor summer coating; they will thicken the candy and make it unusable.

Dipping and Coating

Covering delicious candy centers with your favorite candy coating is fun and easy. Now that you have learned how to temper real chocolate (see page 16), you are ready to dip and coat. If you use summer coating, which does not require tempering (see page 17), the process is even easier.

How to dip and coat:

1. Line a cookie sheet with parchment paper.

2. Melt chocolate or summer coating according to directions on pages 16 and 17.

3. Carefully drop your favorite flavored chilled ball or center into the melted chocolate. When candy center is completely coated, lift it out of melted chocolate with a dipping fork or spoon, gently tapping handle of utensil on the edge of the container to remove excess chocolate.

4. Turn the dipped center gently out of the spoon onto the parchment paper. Allow to set up at room temperature. If you like, decorate candy with a design by drizzling a little melted chocolate on each piece.

Dipped candy can also be rolled in chopped nuts or sprinkles before placing on the parchment to set up.

Candy Mold Care and Use

Candies molded into various shapes are easy and fun to make. You'll find a wide variety of candy molds in candy- and cake-decorating supply stores.

My favorite molds have the designs pressed into a sheet of coated plastic that gives candy a shiny finish and ensures its easy release from the mold. Metal molds can also be used, but finished candy will be dull.

For three-dimensional candies, which have a front and back, you will need molds that have front and back pieces, or left and right side pieces, that clip together. In plastic molds, matching pieces are on one sheet and can be easily cut apart with scissors.

Most candy molds are quite durable, but they do require gentle care. With a little TLC, they will serve you for years.

DO	DO NOT
DO wash molds in warm water and towel dry.	DO NOT use detergent.
DO store molds flat or straight on edge.	DO NOT wash in dishwasher.
	DO NOT wash in hot water.
	DO NOT mold candy that is too hot.

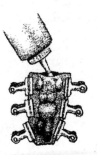

How To Make Candy in Molds

Hint: Use a spoon or squeeze bottle to put summer coating into molds

Flat Molds

For Solid Candies

1. Fill to the top of each shell.

2. Tap mold gently on table or counter to release air bubbles and to make sure candy fills decorative swirl, which will be the top of the finished candy.

3. Place in freezer and chill, usually 3-4 minutes.

4. When chilled thoroughly, turn mold over and tap gently to release candy.

For Filled Candies

1. Fill each shell about 1/3 full of candy.

2. Tap mold gently on table or counter to release air bubbles and to make sure candy fills decorative swirl, which will be the top of the finished candy.

3. Use a small brush about 1/2" wide and brush the candy up the sides of the mold to form the shell for the filling. After brushing the candy up the sides, hold the mold up to the light to make sure you cannot see through the shells. If there are light spots, add a little more candy and paint up the sides again.

continued on following page ☞ ☞ ☞

For Filled Candies *(continued)*

4. Let the candy in the mold set up at room temperature, usually about 5-8 minutes or until it is dull in appearance. Then, roll the filling into balls, or use a spatula or a pastry bag, and insert filling into shells. Leave enough space at the top to put the back of candy on to seal each piece.

5. Put summer coating onto the top of each shell to finish each piece of candy.

6. Tap filled mold gently on table or counter to flatten the back of each candy.

7. Place filled mold in freezer and chill, usually 3-4 minutes.

8. When chilled thoroughly, turn mold over and tap gently on counter top to release candy.

Full Solid, Full Hollow, and Filled Hollow Molding

Molds referred to as "full type" or "hollow" are those that have front and back or right and left sides and make a full or three-dimensional figure when finished.

Lay-on method

1. Use each half as a flat mold.

2. Make two at a time, fill both cavities (front and back) with summer coating or tempered chocolate. Be careful not to overfill. Gently tap out air bubbles.

3. Place molds into freezer and chill, usually 5-8 minutes, or longer if mold is large. It will unmold easily if it is thoroughly chilled.

4. When completely chilled, tap mold gently on table, counter, or on your hand. Allow to warm at room temperature.

5. Fill both cavities again with summer coating or tempered chocolate.

continued on following page ☞ ☞ ☞

Lay-on method (continued)

6. Lay hardened candy on freshly filled counterparts (front on back or right on left). If there is a space between, roll slightly to fill in.

7. Place in freezer and chill, usually 3-5 minutes, or longer if mold is large. Once again, it will unmold easily if it is well chilled.

NOTE: Since you have molded one side at a time, air bubbles can be eliminated by tapping on the table to release them immediately after filling. One of the greatest problems encountered by open bottom molds is air bubbles.

Melted summer coating can be used to adhere royal icing decorations or sprinkles to chocolate pieces.

It is not necessary to wash molds after each use if candy is taken out of mold before completely set. Simply wipe out the mold before continuing.

Full hollow molding

1. Cut to separate front and back or left and right side.

2. Trim edges to within 1/2" of mold so they are aligned.

3. Fill the deepest side of the mold to the top with summer coating or tempered chocolate and tap out air bubbles.

4. Align other half of the mold on the piece with candy in it. Clip together with heavy clips around the edges every 1/2" or so to hold the two pieces together.

5. Roll the clipped mold around and over end to end so entire mold is coated on the inside.

6. Place filled mold in the freezer to chill. It is very important to turn the mold every minute to re-coat the inside of the mold. Usually 3-4 turns are enough, depending on the size of the mold.

7. Remove mold from freezer, undo clips and tap the mold gently in your hand. If chilled enough, candy should drop out easily.

continued on following page ☞ ☞ ☞

Solid mold open bottom

1. Cut mold as above; also cut out bottom of mold, leaving 1/2" edge if possible.

2. Clip both sides of mold together.

3. Hold mold upside down; fill to the top with summer coating or tempered chocolate.

4. Tap out air bubbles.

5. Put filled mold in freezer upside down for 3-5 minutes or longer depending on the size of the mold.

6. Undo clips, take apart. Tap gently in your hand to release candy.

Hollow filled with open bottom

1. Cut as for solid mold open bottom

2. Clip both mold sides together.

3. Hold mold upside down; fill 1/2 full with summer coating or tempered chocolate.

4. Roll chocolate up to the opening to coat the inside of the mold. Repeat rolling until summer coating or tempered chocolate almost stops moving.

5. Allow to set up at room temperature.

6. Put filling in through the bottom opening; fill to within 1/2" of the top; cap with summer coating or tempered chocolate.

7. Put in freezer upside down for 3-5 minutes or longer depending on the size of the mold.

8. Undo the clips and take apart. Tap gently in your hand. If thoroughly chilled, candy should drop out easily.

continued on following page ☞ ☞ ☞

Molding Suckers

1. Pour melted summer coating or tempered chocolate into the mold, filling to top.

2. Tap out air bubbles. Hold the mold up and carefully check to see if all air bubbles are gone.

3. Lay the sucker stick about 1/3 way into the candy and roll it back and forth to coat. Then lay the uncoated end of stick into groove for stick.

4. Place filled mold in the freezer to chill, usually 3-5 minutes, depending on the size of the mold.

5. Take mold out of the freezer and tap gently on table or counter. If thoroughly chilled, suckers should drop out easily.

Candy Painting

It's fun to add color to home-made candies by "painting" them with summer coatings, which come in many different colors and a variety of flavors. Just remember, when using more than one coating, choose flavors that are compatible.

You can create your own colors by using white summer coating and adding candy liquid oil-based colors or candy powdered colors. These are available at cake- and candy supply stores. **Note:** Don't use liquid colors found in grocery stores. These colorings are mostly water, will harden your candy, and you will not be able to melt it down again.

If decorative painting is desired, paint the inside of the mold with melted colored summer coatings where desired. Be sure the colors painted on are thick enough so you can't see through them when the mold is held up to the light. You may want to use a couple of different sized brushes, perhaps a #1 and a #4. When using more than one color, simply wipe the brush off on a clean towel and go to the next color. Remember, do not get water into the candy.

Allow the candy to set up at room temperature. Then, fill the mold with warm candy, and tap mold gently on table or counter to release air bubbles. Chill in the freezer about 3-4 minutes. When thoroughly chilled, turn upside down and tap gently. Candy will fall out.

Summer coating can be remelted and remolded several times.

FUDGE

Rich Cocoa Fudge

This is the recipe your grandmother used to make, and one of my most requested recipes.

 3 cups sugar
 2/3 cup cocoa
 1/8 teaspoon salt
 1 1/2 cups milk
 1/4 cup (1/2 stick) butter or margarine
 1 teaspoon vanilla extract

Line an 8- or 9-inch square pan with foil; butter foil. Set aside.

In a heavy 4-quart saucepan, stir together the sugar, cocoa and salt. Add milk. Cook over medium heat, stirring constantly, until mixture comes to a full rolling boil. Place a candy thermometer into the saucepan. Bulb of candy thermometer should not rest on bottom of saucepan. Boil without stirring to 234 degrees or until syrup, when dropped into very cold water, forms a soft ball which flattens when removed from water. Remove from heat.

Add butter and vanilla. DO NOT STIR. Allow mixture to cool at room temperature until it reaches 110 degrees. Beat with wooden spoon until fudge thickens and loses some of its gloss. Quickly spread into prepared pan. Cool. Cut into squares.

Store in airtight container or plastic wrap in refrigerator.

Yield: About 36 pieces, or 1-3/4 pounds

Nutty Rich Cocoa Fudge

Grandma added a generous portion of her favorite nuts for special occasions.

3 cups sugar
2/3 cup cocoa
1/8 teaspoon salt
1 1/2 cups milk
1/4 cup (1/2 stick) butter or margarine
1 teaspoon vanilla extract
1 cup chopped almonds, pecans or walnuts

Line 8- or 9-inch square pan with foil; butter foil. Set aside.

In a heavy 4-quart saucepan, stir together the sugar, cocoa and salt. Add milk. Cook over medium heat, stirring constantly, until mixture comes to a full rolling boil. Place a candy thermometer into the saucepan. Bulb of candy thermometer should not rest on bottom of saucepan. Boil without stirring to 234 degrees or until syrup, when dropped into very cold water, forms a soft ball which flattens when removed from water. Remove from heat.

Add butter and vanilla. DO NOT STIR. Allow mixture to cool at room temperature until it reaches 110 degrees. Beat with wooden spoon until fudge thickens and loses some of its gloss. Immediately stir in chopped nuts. Quickly spread into prepared pan. Cool. Cut into squares.

Store in plastic wrap or tightly covered container in refrigerator.

Yield: About 36 pieces, or 1-3/4 pounds

Marshmallow-Nut Cocoa Fudge

Marshmallow cream makes old-fashioned fudge thoroughly modern.

3 cups sugar
3/4 cup cocoa
1/8 teaspoon salt
1 1/2 cups milk
1/4 cup (1/2 stick) butter or margarine
1 cup marshmallow cream
1 teaspoon vanilla extract
1 cup chopped walnuts or pecans

Line 8- or 9-inch square pan with foil; butter foil. Set aside.

In a heavy 4-quart saucepan, stir together the sugar, cocoa and salt. Add milk. Cook over medium heat, stirring constantly, until mixture comes to a full rolling boil. Place a candy thermometer into the saucepan and boil, without stirring, to 234 degrees, or until syrup, when dropped into very cold water, forms a soft ball which flattens when removed from water. Remove from heat.

Add butter, marshmallow cream and vanilla. DO NOT STIR. Allow mixture to cool at room temperature until it reaches 110 degrees. Beat with wooden spoon until fudge thickens and loses some of its gloss, approximately 10 minutes. Stir in chopped nuts. Quickly spread into prepared pan. Cool. Cut into squares.

Store in airtight container or in plastic wrap in refrigerator.

Yield: About 36 pieces, or 1-3/4 pounds

Melt-In-Your-Mouth Fudge

This fudge is almost too easy and too delicious to be true.

    1 cup nut meats
    1 pound chocolate
    3 tablespoons butter
    1 14-ounce can sweetened condensed milk

Line an 8-inch square pan with plastic wrap; set aside.

Coarsely chop the nuts; set aside.

Chop the chocolate into 1-inch pieces. Fill the bottom of a double boiler with very hot tap water. Put the chopped chocolate in the top of the double boiler and place over bottom of double boiler. Stir until chocolate is melted.

Remove top of double boiler from bottom, and stir in the sweetened condensed milk and the nuts.

Pour into the prepared pan. Set up at room temperature. When cool, cut into 1-inch squares.

Store in airtight container in refrigerator.

Yield: 64 1-inch pieces

Easy Rocky Road

Use your microwave to whip up a batch of easy and delicious rocky road.

    2 cups (12-ounce package) semi-sweet chocolate chips, or 1 3/4 cups
       (10-ounce package) semi-sweet chocolate chunks
    1/4 cup (1/2 stick) butter or margarine
    2 tablespoons shortening
    3 cups miniature marshmallows
    1/2 cup coarsely chopped nuts

Line 8-inch square pan with foil; set aside.

In large microwave-safe bowl, place chocolate chips, butter and shortening. Microwave at HIGH (100%) for 1 to 1 1/2 minutes, stirring every 20 seconds until chocolate chips are melted and mixture is smooth when stirred.

Add marshmallows and nuts; blend well. Spread evenly in prepared pan. Cover and refrigerate until firm. Cut into 2-inch squares.

Store in airtight container in refrigerator.

Yield: 16 squares

Foolproof Dark Chocolate Fudge

Dark, delicious and as easy as one-two-three.

3 cups (1 1/2 12-ounce packages) semi-sweet chocolate chips
1 can (14 ounces) sweetened condensed milk
Dash salt
1 cup chopped walnuts
1 1/2 teaspoons vanilla extract

Line an 8- or 9-inch square pan with plastic wrap; set aside.

In a heavy saucepan over low heat, melt chips, sweetened condensed milk and salt. Remove from heat; stir in walnuts and vanilla.

Spread evenly into prepared pan. Refrigerate 2 hours or until firm. Remove from pan; place on cutting board. Peel off foil; cut into squares.

Touchdown Chocolate Fudge:

After adding nuts and vanilla, cool 10 to 12 minutes. On foil-lined baking sheet, quickly and gently form into football shape (do not overwork). Refrigerate 2 hours or until firm. Place on serving plate. Garnish as desired.

Store loosely covered at room temperature.

Yield: About 5 dozen pieces, or 2 pounds

Rocky Road Fudge

Football fans will cheer when you bring out the rocky road fudge at your fall tailgate party.

1 pound chocolate
3 tablespoons butter
1 14-ounce can sweetened condensed milk
1 cup miniature marshmallows
1 cup nut meats

Line an 8-inch square pan with plastic wrap; set aside.

Chop the nuts coarsely. Set aside.

Chop the chocolate into 1-inch pieces. Fill the bottom of a double boiler with very hot tap water. Put the chopped chocolate in the top of the double boiler and place over bottom of double boiler. Stir until chocolate is melted.

Remove top of double boiler from the bottom, and stir in the sweetened condensed milk, nuts and marshmallows.

Pour fudge into the prepared pan. Set up at room temperature. When firm, cut into 1-inch squares.

Store in airtight container in refrigerator.

Yield: 64 1-inch squares

White Fudge

For a romantic Valentine's gift, place white fudge in a heart-shaped container or showcase it in shiny red cellophane.

1 1/2 cups granulated sugar
3/4 cups butter
1 cup non-dairy liquid coffee creamer
1 1/2 teaspoons white vinegar
12 ounces white chocolate
2 1/4 cups miniature marshmallows
1 teaspoon vanilla

Line an 8-inch square pan with plastic wrap; set aside.

Chop the chocolate into 1-inch pieces; set aside.

Place the sugar, butter, non-dairy creamer and vinegar into a heavy 3-quart saucepan. Cook without stirring over medium heat. Place a candy thermometer into the saucepan and heat to 238 degrees.

Remove from heat, and add the marshmallows and vanilla. Stir with a wooden spoon until marshmallows are almost melted. Add the chopped chocolate. Stir until the chocolate is melted.

Pour and spread flat in the prepared pan. Allow to set up at room temperature, or chill in refrigerator.

When firm, cut into 1-inch squares.

Store in airtight container in refrigerator.

Yield: 64 1-inch pieces

Golden Maple Fudge

Long before Europeans arrived in the New World, Native Americans were enjoying the flavor of maple. It's still a favorite today, especially when combined with modern additions like golden raisins, butterscotch chips, and marshmallow cream.

1 1/2 cups firmly packed light brown sugar
1/2 cup granulated sugar
1/3 cup butter
1/2 cup whipping cream
2 1/4 cups marshmallow cream
1 1/4 cups butterscotch chips
3/4 cup pecans
1/3 cup golden raisins
1 teaspoon vanilla
1 teaspoon maple flavoring

Line an 8-inch square pan with plastic wrap; set aside.

Coarsely chop the pecans; set aside.

Place the sugars, butter, and whipping cream in a heavy 4-quart saucepan over medium heat. Stir constantly with a wooden spoon until the butter melts. Place a candy thermometer into the saucepan and heat to 238 degrees.

Remove from heat, and add the marshmallow cream. Stir until the marshmallow is almost melted. Add the butterscotch chips. Stir until chips are melted. Add the pecans, raisins, vanilla and maple flavoring.

Pour into the prepared pan. Set up at room temperature for several hours. Cut into 1-inch squares.

Store in airtight container in refrigerator.

Yield: 64 1-inch pieces

Peanut Butter Fudge Cut-Outs

Use your microwave and this fudge will be ready for the cookie cutters in record time.

3 1/3 cups (2 10-ounce packages) peanut butter chips
1 can (14 ounces) sweetened condensed milk
Dash salt
1 cup chopped walnuts (optional)
1 1/2 teaspoons vanilla extract

Line 13 X 9 X 2-inch pan with plastic wrap, extending over edges of pan. Set aside.

In large microwave-safe bowl, place peanut butter chips, sweetened condensed milk and salt. Microwave at HIGH (100%) 1 minute; stir. Stirring every 20 seconds, microwave an additional 15 to 30 seconds, or just until chips are melted and mixture is smooth when stirred.

Stir in walnuts, if desired, and vanilla. Immediately spread evenly in prepared pan. Refrigerate 2 hours or until firm. Turn out onto cutting board, and peel off plastic wrap. With small cookie-cutters, cut into favorite shapes.

Conventional Directions:

In heavy saucepan over low heat, melt chips with sweetened condensed milk and salt. Remove from heat; stir in walnuts, if desired, and vanilla. Spread evenly into prepared pan.

Store tightly covered in cool, dry place.

Yield: About 2 pounds

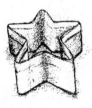

Butterscotch Fudge Cut-Outs

This speedy microwave recipe is perfect for butterscotch lovers.

3 1/3 cups (2 10-ounce packages) butterscotch chips
1 can (14 ounces) sweetened condensed milk
Dash salt
1 cup chopped walnuts (optional)
1 1/2 teaspoons vanilla extract

Line 13 X 9 X 2-inch pan with plastic wrap, extending over edges of pan. Set aside.

In large microwave-safe bowl, place butterscotch chips, sweetened condensed milk and salt. Microwave at HIGH (100%) 1 minute. Stirring every 20 seconds, microwave an additional 15 to 30 seconds, or just until chips are melted and mixture is smooth when stirred.

Stir in walnuts, if desired, and vanilla. Immediately spread evenly in prepared pan. Refrigerate 2 hours or until firm. Turn out onto cutting board and peel off plastic wrap. With small cookie-cutters, cut into favorite shapes.

Conventional Directions:

In heavy saucepan over low heat, melt chips with sweetened condensed milk and salt. Remove from heat; stir in walnuts, if desired, and vanilla. Spread evenly into prepared pan.

Store tightly covered in cool, dry place.

Yield: About 2 pounds

Foolproof Fudge Cut-Outs

Use your microwave. This foolproof fudge is easy, fast, and fun!

3 cups (1 1/2 12-ounce packages) semi-sweet chocolate chips
1 can (14 ounces) sweetened condensed milk
Dash salt
1 cup chopped walnuts (optional)
1 1/2 teaspoons vanilla extract

Line 13 X 9 X 2-inch pan with plastic wrap, extending over edges of pan. Set aside.

In large microwave-safe bowl, place chocolate chips, sweetened condensed milk and salt. Microwave at HIGH (100%) 1 minute. Stirring every 20 seconds, microwave an additional 15 to 30 seconds, or just until chips are melted and mixture is smooth when stirred.

Stir in walnuts, if desired, and vanilla. Immediately spread evenly in prepared pan. Refrigerate 2 hours or until firm. Turn out onto cutting board and peel off plastic wrap. With small cookie-cutters, cut into favorite shapes.

Conventional Directions:

In heavy saucepan over low heat, melt chips with sweetened condensed milk and salt. Remove from heat; stir in walnuts, if desired, and vanilla. Spread evenly into prepared pan.

Store tightly covered in cool, dry place.

Yield: About 2 pounds

Layered Mint Chocolate Fudge

A touch of the green is the perfect thing for St. Patrick's Day.

1 pound milk or dark chocolate
1 14-ounce can sweetened condensed milk
5 tablespoons butter
1 teaspoon vanilla
8 ounces white chocolate chips or white chocolate
2 teaspoons peppermint flavoring, OR 1/4 teaspoon peppermint oil
3 to 5 drops green or red food coloring (optional)

Line an 8-inch square pan with plastic wrap. Set aside.

Chop the dark and white chocolates into 1-inch pieces. Fill the bottoms of two double boilers with very hot tap water. Put the chopped chocolates in the tops of separate double boilers and place over the bottoms. Add 4 tablespoons of the butter to the dark chocolate and 1 tablespoon of the butter to the white chocolate. Stir until the chocolates are melted and the butter is incorporated.

Remove the double boiler top containing the dark chocolate from the hot water. Add 1 cup of the sweetened condensed milk and the vanilla to this mixture, and stir well. Pour half of this mixture into the prepared pan. Place remaining dark chocolate mixture back over the hot water.

Remove the double boiler top containing the white chocolate. Add remaining sweetened condensed milk, peppermint flavoring and food coloring. Stir well. Spread over the layer of dark chocolate. Chill 5 to 8 minutes. Spread the remaining dark chocolate mixture over the mint layer. Chill until firm. Cut into 1-inch squares.

Store in an airtight container in the refrigerator.

Yield: 64 1-inch pieces

Creamy Double Decker Fudge

A microwave miracle! Made with easy to use sweetened condensed milk, this peanut butter and chocolate fudge requires no candy thermometer and is smooth and creamy every time.

> 1 cup peanut butter chips
> 1 can (14 ounces) sweetened condensed milk, divided
> 1 teaspoon vanilla extract, divided
> 1 cup semi-sweet chocolate chips

Line 8-inch square pan with plastic wrap; set aside.

In a small microwave-safe bowl, place peanut butter chips and 2/3 cup of the sweetened condensed milk. Microwave at HIGH (100%) for 1 to 1 1/2 minutes, stirring every 20 seconds, until chips are melted and mixture is smooth when stirred. Stir in 1/2 teaspoon vanilla; spread evenly into prepared pan.

In small microwave-safe bowl, place remaining sweetened condensed milk and chocolate chips; repeat above microwave procedure. Stir in remaining 1/2 teaspoon vanilla; spread evenly over peanut butter layer. Cover; refrigerate until firm. Cut into 1-inch squares.

Store in an airtight container in the refrigerator.

Yield: About 4 dozen squares or 1 1/2 pounds

Peanut Butter Fudge I

Marshmallows, butterscotch chips, and chunky peanut butter make a creamy, crunchy fudge.

3 tablespoons butter
3/4 cup evaporated milk
1 2/3 cups granulated sugar
1/8 teaspoon salt
2 1/4 cups miniature marshmallows
1 6-ounce package butterscotch chips
1 3/4 cups chunky peanut butter
1 1/2 teaspoons vanilla
1 6-ounce package semi-sweet chocolate chips
1 teaspoon butter
1 teaspoon evaporated milk

Line an 8-inch square pan with plastic wrap; set aside.

Place the 3 tablespoons of butter, the 3/4 cup evaporated milk, sugar and salt in a heavy 3-quart saucepan. Cook over medium heat, stirring constantly with a wooden spoon, until mixture boils. Continue stirring constantly, and boil for 5 minutes.

Remove from heat. Add marshmallows and stir until most of the marshmallows are melted. Add the butterscotch chips, peanut butter and vanilla. Stir until completely melted. Pour into the prepared pan and spread evenly.

Melt the chocolate chips and the 1 teaspoon butter in a small saucepan over very low heat. Remove from heat and add the 1 teaspoon evaporated milk. Stir until mixture starts to thicken. Spread over peanut butter mixture. Refrigerate until firm. Cut into 1-inch squares.

Store in an airtight container or plastic wrap in the refrigerator.

Yield: 64 1-inch pieces

Peanut Butter Fudge II

Peanut butter chips and marshmallow cream give you a wonderfully smooth peanut butter fudge.

1 2/3 cups peanut butter chips
2 1/4 cups sugar
1 jar (7-ounces) marshmallow cream
3/4 cup evaporated milk
1/4 cup (1/2 stick) butter or margarine
1 teaspoon vanilla extract

Line 8-inch square pan with foil, extending foil over edges of pan. Set aside. Place peanut butter chips into large bowl and set aside.

In heavy 3-quart saucepan, combine sugar, marshmallow cream, evaporated milk and butter. Cook over medium heat, stirring constantly, until mixture boils. Boil for 5 minutes, stirring.

Remove from heat; stir in vanilla. Allow to set for 4 minutes. Stir the hot mixture into peanut butter chips until chips are completely melted; quickly pour into prepared pan.

Cool in refrigerator for 1 1/2 hours or until firm. Remove from pan; place on cutting board. Peel off foil; cut into 1-inch squares.

Store in an airtight container in the refrigerator.

Yield: About 5 dozen pieces or about 2 pounds

Butterscotch Fudge

This tasty fudge will have your lassies and laddies dancing the Highland fling.

    1/2 cup butter
    2 tablespoons light corn syrup
    1 1/4 cups light brown sugar
    1 1/4 cups granulated sugar
    1 cup sour cream
    1 1/2 teaspoons vanilla
    1 cup nut meats
    1 6-ounce package butterscotch chips

Line an 8-inch square pan with plastic wrap; set aside.

Chop the nuts to medium fine; set aside.

Fill the bottom of a double boiler with very hot tap water. Put the butterscotch chips in the top of the double boiler and place over bottom of double boiler. Stir until chips are melted.

Melt the butter in a heavy 4-quart saucepan over medium heat. Add the brown sugar. Stir with a wooden spoon and cook to boiling. Add the granulated sugar, corn syrup and sour cream. Cook over medium heat until the sugar dissolves. Place a candy thermometer into the saucepan and heat to 236 degrees. Remove from heat. Let cool at room temperature until lukewarm. Do not stir while mixture is cooling.

Add the melted chips to the lukewarm mixture. Pour into a large mixing bowl, and beat until mixture holds its shape and is not glossy. Add the vanilla and nuts, and quickly pour into the prepared pan. Cool and cut into 1-inch squares.

Store in an airtight container.

Yield: 64 1-inch pieces

Foolproof Chocolate Fudge

Foolproof fudge is a perfect gift so be sure to keep plenty of chocolate chips and miniature marshmallows on hand for those special occasions.

1 3/4 cups granulated sugar
3/4 cup evaporated milk
1 12-ounce package semi-sweet chocolate chips
1 2/3 cups miniature marshmallows
1/8 teaspoon salt
6 tablespoons butter, room temperature
1 1/2 nut meats

Line an 8-inch square pan with plastic wrap; set aside.

Chop the nuts coarsely. Cut the butter into small pieces. Place the marshmallows, salt, butter and nuts in a large bowl.

Place the sugar and milk in a heavy 3-quart saucepan. Cook over medium heat, stirring constantly with a wooden spoon until the sugar is dissolved and mixture comes to a boil. Boil and stir, cooking 5 minutes.

Remove from heat; stir in vanilla. Allow to stand 4 minutes. Pour hot mixture over remaining ingredients and stir until chips are melted. Quickly pour into prepared pan. Let cool, and cut into 1-inch squares.

Store in an airtight container or plastic wrap in the refrigerator.

Yield: 64 1-inch pieces

Chocolate Fudge

Blend semi-sweet chocolate chips and marshmallow cream for a rich, easy-to-make fudge.

2 cups semi-sweet chocolate chips
2 1/4 cups sugar
1 jar (7-ounces) marshmallow cream
3/4 cup evaporated milk
1/4 cup (1/2 stick) butter or margarine
1 teaspoon vanilla extract

Line 8-inch square pan with foil, extending foil over edges of pan. Set aside.

Put chocolate chips into a large bowl. Set aside.

In heavy 3-quart saucepan, combine sugar, marshmallow cream, evaporated milk and butter. Cook over medium heat, stirring constantly, until mixture boils. Boil for 5 minutes, stirring.

Remove from heat; stir in vanilla. Allow to stand for 4 minutes. Stir hot mixture into chocolate chips until chips are completely melted. Quickly pour into prepared pan.

Cool in refrigerator for 1 1/2 hours or until firm. Remove from pan; place on cutting board. Peel off foil; cut into 1-inch squares.

Store in an airtight container in the refrigerator.

Yield: About 5 dozen pieces or about 2 pounds

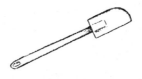

Chocolate Cherry Yummies

Cherry-marshmallow filling nestles between layers of peanutty chocolate. Yum!

1 pound milk chocolate
3/4 cup peanut butter
1 pound roasted peanuts

Line a 9- X 13-inch cookie sheet with plastic wrap and set aside. Chop the nuts finely. Chop the chocolate into 1-inch pieces. Melt the chocolate and peanut butter over low heat in a heavy 2-quart saucepan. Remove from heat and stir in the peanuts. Pour half of this mixture into the prepared pan and chill in the refrigerator until set. Meanwhile, prepare the Cherry Center.

Cherry Center:

2 cups granulated sugar
2/3 cup evaporated milk
1/2 cup butter
12 large marshmallows
12 ounces pink cherry chips
1 teaspoon cherry flavoring
1 teaspoon vanilla

Place sugar, evaporated milk and butter into a heavy 4-quart saucepan. Melt over medium heat, stirring constantly with a wooden spoon. Bring this mixture to a boil, and boil for 5 minutes.

Remove from heat and add the marshmallows, stirring until they are dissolved. Add the cherry chips, cherry flavoring and vanilla. Stir until melted.

Spread this mixture over the cooled chocolate-peanut layer and return to refrigerator for 15 minutes. Then spread the remaining chocolate-peanut mixture over the cherry layer and chill. Cut into 1 1/2-inch squares.

Store in an airtight container.

Yield: 80 pieces

Double Decker Fudge

Flavorful layers of peanut butter and chocolate result in doubly delightful fudge.

    1 cup peanut butter chips
    1 cup semi-sweet chocolate chips
    2 1/4 cups sugar
    1 jar (7-ounces) marshmallow cream
    3/4 cup evaporated milk
    1/4 cup (1/2 stick) butter or margarine
    1 teaspoon vanilla extract

Line 8-inch square pan with foil, extending foil over edges of pan. Set aside.

Measure peanut butter chips into one medium bowl and chocolate chips into second medium bowl. Set aside.

In heavy 3-quart saucepan, combine sugar, marshmallow cream, evaporated milk and butter. Cook over medium heat, stirring constantly, until mixture boils. Boil for 5 minutes, stirring.

Remove from heat; stir in vanilla. Allow to stand for 4 minutes. Stir in half of the hot mixture (1 1/2 cups) into peanut butter chips, until chips are completely melted; quickly pour into prepared pan.

Stir remaining half of hot mixture into chocolate chips until chips are completely melted. Quickly spread over top of peanut butter layer.

Cool in refrigerator for 1 1/2 hours or until firm. Remove from pan; place on cutting board. Peel off foil; cut into 1-inch squares.

Store in an airtight container in the refrigerator.

Yield: About 5 dozen pieces or about 2 pounds

Chocolate Almond Fudge

Many people have known this candy as Million Dollar Fudge.

        4 cups sugar
        1 jar (7 ounces) marshmallow cream
        1 1/2 cups (12-ounce can) evaporated milk
        1 tablespoon butter or margarine
        2 cups (12-ounce package) semi-sweet chocolate chips
        1 (7 ounce) milk chocolate bar, broken into pieces
        1 teaspoon vanilla extract
        3/4 cup slivered almonds, toasted and coarsely chopped

Line 9-inch square pan with foil; set aside.

To toast almonds, heat oven to 350 degrees. Spread almonds in thin layer in shallow baking pan. Bake for 5- to 10 minutes, stirring occasionally, until light golden brown. Cool and set aside.

In heavy 4-quart saucepan, stir together sugar, marshmallow cream, evaporated milk and butter. Cook over medium heat, stirring constantly, until mixture comes to full rolling boil. Boil, stirring constantly, for 7 minutes.

Remove from heat. Allow to stand for 4 minutes. Add chocolate chips and chocolate bar pieces, stirring until chocolate is melted and mixture is smooth. Stir in vanilla and almonds.

Pour into prepared pan; cool until firm. Cut into 1-inch squares.

Store in an airtight container.

Yield: About 5 dozen squares, or about 4 pounds

Ultra Semi-Sweet Fudge Cut-Outs

For the ultimate in fudge cut-outs, try this rich, easy-to-make microwave recipe.

3 1/3 cups (2 10-ounce packages) semi-sweet chocolate chunks
1 can (14 ounces) sweetened condensed milk
Dash salt
1 cup chopped walnuts (optional)
1 1/2 teaspoons vanilla extract

Line 13 X 9 X 2-inch pan with plastic wrap, extending over edges of pan. Set aside.

In large microwave-safe bowl, place chocolate chunks, sweetened condensed milk and salt. Microwave at HIGH (100%) 1 minute. Stirring every 20 seconds, microwave an additional 15 to 30 seconds, or just until chunks are melted and mixture is smooth when stirred.

Stir in walnuts, if desired, and vanilla. Immediately spread evenly in prepared pan. Refrigerate 2 hours or until firm. Turn out onto cutting board and peel off plastic wrap. With small cookie-cutters, cut into favorite shapes.

CONVENTIONAL DIRECTIONS:

In heavy saucepan over low heat, melt chocolate chunks with sweetened condensed milk and salt. Remove from heat; stir in walnuts, if desired, and vanilla. Spread evenly into prepared pan.

Store tightly covered in cool, dry place.

Yield: About 2 pounds

Pliable Fudge #1

Pliable fudge is perfect for rolling or molding into unique shapes. And it's so easy.

       1 pound white or milk chocolate
       1/3 cup corn syrup

Chop the chocolate into 1-inch pieces. Fill the bottom of a double boiler with very hot tap water. Put the chopped chocolate in the top of the double boiler and place over bottom of double boiler. Stir until chocolate is melted.

In separate saucepan, heat the light corn syrup on medium heat until it is lukewarm. Stir into the melted chocolate, and mix well.

Wrap in plastic wrap and allow to set up at room temperature for at least 24 hours.

This pliable fudge is easier to work with the longer it sets. When you are ready to use the pliable fudge, knead a small piece to make it pliable for molding or rolling. To speed the softening process, pliable fudge can be placed in the microwave on medium for 2 to 3 seconds.

Store in airtight container in refrigerator for up to one month.

Yield: Approximately 2 cups

Pliable Fudge #2

You'll want to try several versions of pliable fudge to see which you like best.

      1 pound white or dark chocolate
      10 1/2 ounces sweetened condensed milk

Chop the chocolate into 1-inch pieces. Fill the bottom of a double boiler with very hot tap water. Put the chopped chocolate in the top of the double boiler and place over bottom of double boiler. Stir until chocolate is melted.

Remove from heat and stir in the sweetened condensed milk. Allow mixture to set up at room temperature.

When ready to use the pliable fudge, knead a small piece to make it pliable for molding or rolling. This can be put in the microwave on medium for 2 to 3 seconds to start the softening process prior to kneading.

Wrap in plastic wrap. Store in airtight container in refrigerator for up to one month.

Yield: Approximately 2 cups

Penuche

Dipped in chocolate, this classic fudgelike confection is superb.

1 1/2 cups granulated sugar
1/2 cup firmly packed light brown sugar
1/2 cup heavy whipping cream
1/2 cup non-dairy liquid coffee creamer
3 tablespoons light corn syrup
1 pound milk or dark chocolate for dipping

Before you begin, place a large mixing bowl and beaters in the freezer to chill.

Line a cookie sheet with parchment paper and set aside.

Place the granulated sugar, brown sugar, whipping cream, coffee creamer and corn syrup in a heavy 4-quart saucepan over medium heat. Stir with a wooden spoon. Insert a candy thermometer into the saucepan and cook to 240 degrees, stirring constantly.

Pour into the chilled mixing bowl and place in the refrigerator. Stir every 10 minutes until the mixture is cool. Remove bowl and mix with chilled beaters until the mixture holds its shape.

Roll into 3/4-inch balls. Place on the prepared cookie sheet and chill for 5 to 8 minutes.

Chop the chocolate into 1-inch pieces. Fill the bottom of a double boiler with very hot tap water. Put the chopped chocolate in the top pan and place over bottom. Stir until chocolate is melted.

Using a dipping fork or dipping spoon, dip rolled mixture into the melted chocolate, and place back onto the prepared cookie sheet to set up.

Store in a covered container.

Yield: 48

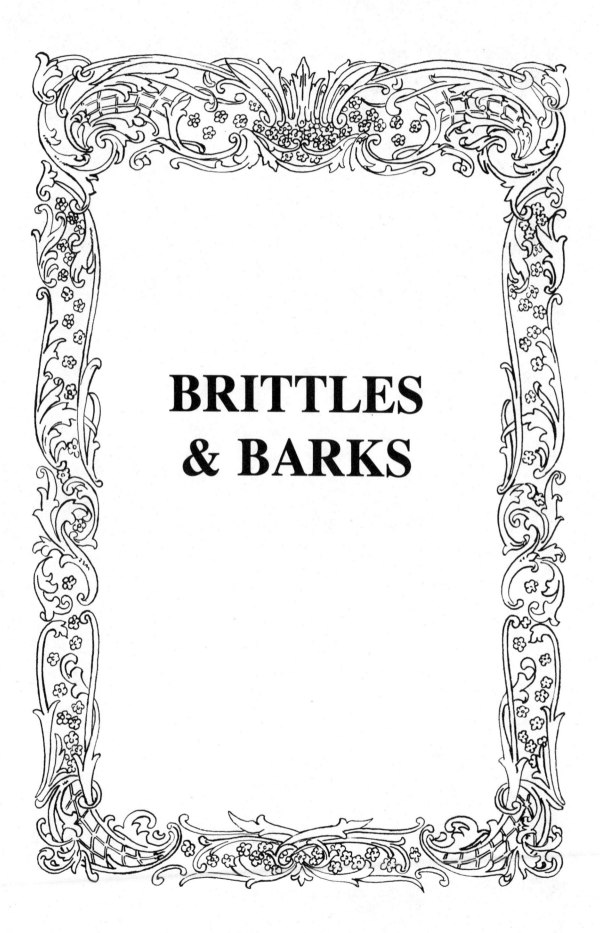

BRITTLES
& BARKS

Peanut Brittle

Although peanuts have been enjoyed for thousands of years, only modern generations have had the sublime pleasure of eating peanut brittle.

   2 1/2 cups light corn syrup
   2 cups granulated sugar
   1 cup water
   2 cups raw peanuts (available at health food stores)
   2 teaspoons baking soda

Generously butter a 12- X 16-inch cookie sheet or jelly roll pan. Set aside. Sift the baking soda and set aside.

Place the corn syrup, sugar and water in a heavy 4-quart saucepan. Bring to a boil. Add the raw peanuts and a candy thermometer. Heat, stirring constantly with a wooden spoon, to 300 degrees. Cooking goes very quickly from 295 to 300 degrees, so once 295 is reached, watch mixture closely.

Remove from heat, and stir in the sifted baking soda. Stir until mixture becomes foamy.

Pour as thin as possible onto prepared cookie sheet. Allow to cool at room temperature. When set, crack into pieces.

Store in an airtight container.

Yield: About 2 pounds

Coconut Mixed Nut Brittle

Flaked coconut adds an exotic island touch to this yummy peanut brittle.

    1 can mixed nuts (no peanuts)
    2 teaspoons soda
    3 cups light corn syrup
    2 1/2 cup granulated sugar
    1 cup water
    1/2 cup butter
    1 cup raw peanuts (available at health food stores)
    1 3/4 cups wide flake coconut (available at health food stores)

Preheat oven to 225 degrees. Place the canned mixed nuts in a 9- X 13-inch pan, ready to put into the preheated oven. Generously butter a jelly roll pan and set aside. Sift the soda, and set aside.

Place the corn syrup, sugar, water and butter in a heavy 4-quart saucepan. Bring to a boil over medium-high heat, stirring occasionally with a wooden spoon. Add the raw peanuts.

Place a candy thermometer into the saucepan and heat to 280 degrees. When candy mixture reaches 280 degrees, place the mixed nuts into the oven. Continue to heat over medium-high heat to 285 degrees, and add the coconut, stirring constantly. Once mixture reaches 295 degrees, it will quickly increase to 300, so watch closely. When mixture reaches 300, remove from the heat. Stir in the warm mixed nuts and the sifted baking soda. The soda will make the mixture foamy and airy.

Pour onto the prepared pan, and spread as thin as possible. Allow to set up at room temperature. When set, crack into pieces.

Store in an airtight container.

Yield: 2 1/2 pounds

Buttery Cashew Brittle

Real butter and crunchy cashews create an unforgettable flavor.

1 pound raw cashews (available at health food stores)
2 1/2 cups granulated sugar
2 1/2 cups light corn syrup
1 1/4 cups butter (do not substitute margarine)
3/4 cup water
1 1/2 teaspoons baking soda

Preheat oven to 225 degrees. Place the raw nuts in a 9- X 13-inch cake pan and keep handy.

Sift the baking soda. Set aside.

Generously butter a cookie sheet or jelly roll pan. Set aside.

Place the sugar, corn syrup, butter and water in a heavy 4-quart saucepan. Stir with a wooden spoon. Place a candy thermometer into the saucepan and heat to 260 degrees. At this point, place the nuts in the preheated oven for about 5 minutes. Continue stirring syrup mixture until candy thermometer reaches 275 degrees.

Add the heated nuts to the syrup mixture. Continue stirring until temperature reaches 295 degrees. Remove from heat and stir in the sifted baking soda until mixture becomes foamy.

Pour into the prepared cookie sheet and spread as thin as possible. Set up at room temperature. When cool, crack into pieces.

Store in an airtight container.

Yield: About 3 1/2 pounds

Macadamia Nut Brittle

The macadamia nut originated in Australia and is named after John Macadam, (1827-65), a Scottish-born Australian chemist. Whether Mr. Macadam ever tasted macadamia nut brittle, I cannot say.

3/4 pound macadamia nuts
1 cup butter (do not substitute margarine)
1 cup granulated sugar
1/2 cup light corn syrup
1 cup semi-sweet chocolate chips

Generously butter a cookie sheet; set aside.

Chop the nuts coarsely.

In a heavy 10- to 12-inch skillet, heat the nuts, butter, sugar and corn syrup over low heat. Stir with a wooden spoon until the butter melts and the sugar is dissolved. Increase heat to medium, stir and bring to a boil. Cook the mixture until it turns a golden brown and begins to mass together, approximately 5 to 8 minutes.

Pour onto the prepared cookie sheet. Spread as thin as possible.

Sprinkle the chocolate chips over the top, let the chips melt, and spread evenly over the top of the brittle. Set up at room temperature.

When cool, remove from cookie sheet and break into pieces.

Store in an airtight container.

Yield: 1 1/2 pounds

English Toffee

Classic toffee is especially good when topped with rich dark chocolate.

1/2 pound almonds
3/4 pound dark chocolate
2 cups butter (do not substitute margarine)
2 2/3 cups granulated sugar
1/3 cup water
1/4 cup light corn syrup

Roast the almonds in a 9- X 13-inch cake pan for 10 minutes in a 325 degree oven. Shake the pan a couple of times to stir the nuts. Let the nuts cool, and chop them finely by hand or in a food processor.

Chop the chocolate into 1-inch pieces. Fill the bottom of a double boiler with very hot tap water. Put the chopped chocolate in the top of the double boiler and place over bottom of double boiler. Stir until chocolate is melted.

Generously butter a 12- X 16-inch cookie sheet or jelly roll pan. Set aside.

Place the butter, sugar, water and corn syrup in a heavy 4-quart saucepan over medium heat. Place a candy thermometer into the saucepan and heat to 300 degrees, stirring constantly with a wooden spoon. Remove from heat and pour into the prepared pan. Spread to 1/4-inch thick. Allow to cool.

Pour half the melted chocolate over cooled mixture and spread to the edges. Sprinkle with half the chopped almonds. Allow to set up.

When set, turn out onto parchment paper and spread the other half of the melted chocolate over the toffee. Sprinkle with remaining nuts. When toffee is set up, crack into pieces.

Store in an airtight container.

Yield: 3 1/4 pounds

Almond Bark

Thin and crisp, easy-to-make bark is a nibbling delight.

1 pound white or dark chocolate
1 pound almonds
2 teaspoons vegetable oil

Line a cookie sheet with parchment paper and set aside.

Roast the almonds in a 9- X 13-inch cake pan in a 325 degree oven for 8 to 10 minutes. Allow to cool at room temperature.

Chop the chocolate into 1-inch pieces. Fill the bottom of a double boiler with very hot tap water. Put the chopped chocolate and the vegetable oil in the top of the double boiler and place over bottom of double boiler. Stir until chocolate is melted and oil is incorporated.

Remove top of double boiler from bottom and stir in the roasted almonds. Pour onto the prepared cookie sheet and spread as thin as possible. Allow to harden. Break into pieces.

Store in an airtight container.

Yield: 2 pounds

Crunchy Lemon Bark

Tint this bark or leave it white. Either way, it's ideal for spring bridal showers and luncheons.

 1 pound white chocolate
 2 teaspoons vegetable oil
 1/2 cup hard lemon candy
 1/4 teaspoon yellow food color (optional)
 1/2 teaspoon lemon flavoring, OR 1/8 teaspoon lemon oil

Line a 9- X 13-inch pan with parchment paper. Set aside. Crush the lemon candy in a plastic bag.

Chop the white chocolate into 1-inch pieces. Fill the bottom of a double boiler with very hot tap water. Put the chopped chocolate in the top of the double boiler and place over bottom of double boiler. Stir until chocolate is melted.

Add the oil, food coloring, crushed lemon candy and flavoring to the melted chocolate. Stir to combine.

Pour the mixture into the prepared pan, and spread smooth. Allow to set up at room temperature until firm, but not too hard, approximately 10 minutes. Run the tines of a fork over the surface to make it look like bark. Score in 1 1/2-inch squares. Let harden at room temperature. Cut or break along scores.

Store in an airtight container.

Yield: 24 1 1/2-inch pieces

Marbled Bark

Pink and white swirls make this candy visually appealing as well as delicious.

1 1/4 pound white chocolate
3 teaspoons vegetable oil
2-3 drops red food coloring
1/4 teaspoon peppermint flavoring, OR 1/8 teaspoon peppermint oil
    (or flavoring and coloring of your choice)

Line a 12- X 16-inch cookie sheet with parchment paper; set aside.

Using two double boilers, place 3/4 pound of the white chocolate and 2 teaspoons of the vegetable oil in the top of one double boiler, and the remaining chocolate and oil in the second. Fill the bottoms of the double boilers with very hot tap water. Stir until chocolate is melted.

Remove both from heat. Pour the 3/4 pound mixture into the prepared cookie sheet, and spread smooth.

Add the flavoring and coloring to the remaining 1/2 pound. Pour colored mixture over the white in a zig-zag pattern; then swirl with a knife or spatula. Allow to set up, but not harden, at room temperature, approximately 10 minutes. Score into 1 1/2-inch squares. Allow to harden, and break into pre-scored pieces.

Store in an airtight container.

Yield: 55 pieces

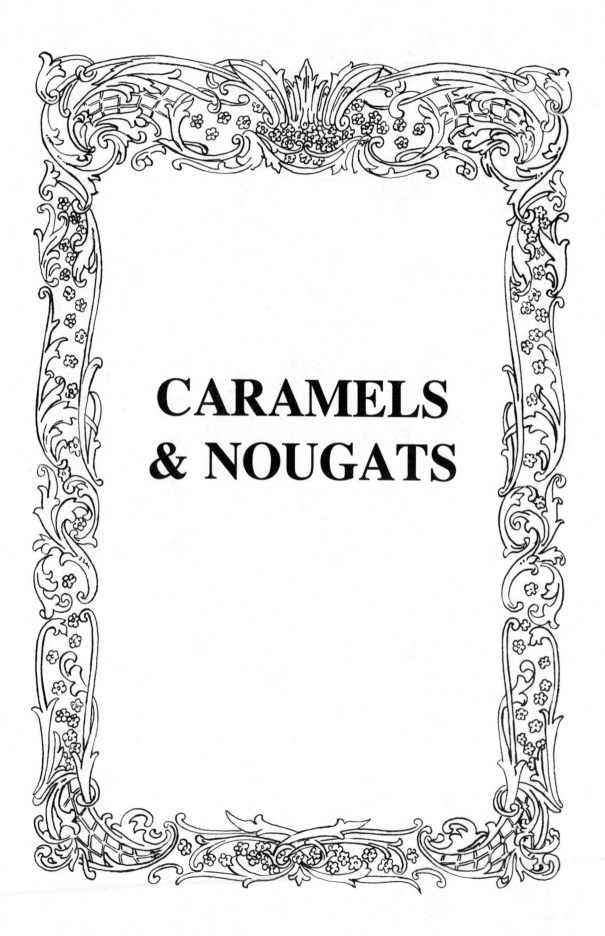

CARAMELS
& NOUGATS

Chocolate Caramels

Smooth, chewy, and sweet with chocolate. Make them today, chill them overnight, and enjoy them tomorrow.

    1 cup light corn syrup
    1 cup granulated sugar
    1 cup sweetened condensed milk
    1 3/4 cups whipping cream
    1/3 cup butter
    3 ounces unsweetened chocolate

Line an 8-inch square pan with foil, and butter it generously. Set aside.

Chop the unsweetened chocolate into 1-inch pieces. Set aside.

Place the corn syrup, sugar, milk, cream and butter in a heavy 4-quart saucepan. Heat over medium heat and stir constantly with a wooden spoon, until sugar has dissolved and mixture is smooth.

Place a candy thermometer into the saucepan and heat to 225 degrees. Slowly add the chopped chocolate. Heat to 243 degrees.

Remove from heat and pour mixture into the prepared pan.

Let cool overnight. When set, cut into 1-inch squares.

These can be also used as the caramel in molded chocolates, or dipped in melted chocolate.

Store in plastic wrap.

Yield: 64 caramels

Cream Nut Caramels

Finely chopped pecans and rich cream make this candy sensational.

3/4 cup pecans
2 cups heavy cream
1 3/4 cups granulated sugar
1/4 cup light brown sugar
1 cup light corn syrup
1/4 cup butter
1/4 teaspoon salt
1 teaspoon vanilla

Measure all ingredients before you begin.

Line an 8-inch square pan with foil and butter it generously. Set aside.

Finely chop the pecans. Set aside

Using a small saucepan, heat the heavy cream until warm.

Remove 1 cup of the warm cream, and place it into a heavy 4-quart saucepan. Add the sugar and corn syrup to the cream in the 4-quart saucepan. Heat on medium for about 5 minutes, stirring with a wooden spoon, until mixture begins to boil. Add the remaining cream very slowly, so the boiling does not stop. Cook about 5 minutes more.

Place a candy thermometer into the saucepan and heat to 230 degrees. Lower the heat to prevent scorching. Add the butter slowly, and heat to 245 degrees.

Remove the candy from the heat, and stir in the salt, vanilla and chopped pecans. Pour mixture into the prepared pan. Allow to set up at room temperature until firm. Cut into 1-inch squares.

Store in plastic wrap.

Yield: 64 1-inch pieces

Caramel-Coconut Roll Ups

Be prepared for praises when you serve creamy caramels with coconut centers.

3/4 cup butter
2 cups brown sugar, firmly packed
Pinch of salt
3/4 cup light corn syrup
1 14-ounce can sweetened condensed milk
1/2 teaspoon vanilla

Line a 9- X 13-inch pan with foil and butter it generously. Set aside.

In a heavy 4-quart saucepan, melt the butter over medium heat. Using a wooden spoon, stir in sugar, salt and corn syrup until dissolved. Then, add the sweetened condensed milk. Place a candy thermometer into the saucepan and, stirring constantly, heat to 243 degrees. Remove from heat; stir in vanilla. Pour into prepared pan and let cool.

Meanwhile, prepare the coconut center.

1 14-ounce can sweetened condensed milk
8 ounces macaroon coconut
1 teaspoon vanilla
1/2 cup light corn syrup
1 pound confectioners sugar

Place sweetened condensed milk, coconut, vanilla and corn syrup into a large mixing bowl. Mix on low until incorporated. Gradually add the confectioners sugar and mix on low speed for 2 to 3 minutes. Place in the refrigerator to allow mixture to set up, and it reaches room temperature.

When caramel is cool, turn out onto a greased surface. Spread the coconut center evenly over the top of the caramel. Roll tightly together, starting at the wide end. Stretch and roll to 2 or 3 inches diameter. Slice into 1-inch pieces.

Store wrapped in plastic wrap.

Yield: 70 1-inch pieces

Time Saving Caramels

In a hurry? Try this quick-as-a-wink caramel recipe.

    3/4 cup butter
    2 cups brown sugar, firmly packed
    Pinch of salt
    3/4 cup light corn syrup
    1 14-ounce can sweetened condensed milk
    1/2 teaspoon vanilla

Line a 9-inch square pan with foil and butter it generously. Set aside.

In a heavy 4-quart saucepan, melt the butter over medium heat. Using a wooden spoon, stir in sugar, salt and corn syrup until dissolved. Then, add the sweetened condensed milk. Place a candy thermometer into the saucepan and, stirring constantly, heat to 243 degrees.

Remove from heat. Stir in vanilla. Pour into prepared pan. Allow to set up overnight at room temperature.

When set, cut into squares.

If desired, dip in melted milk- or dark chocolate.

Store wrapped in plastic wrap.

Yield: 72 1-inch pieces

Vanilla Nougat

Basic nougat takes on exciting new dimensions when you add white chocolate.

8 ounces white chocolate
3 large egg whites, at room temperature
2 3/4 cups light corn syrup
1 1/3 cups granulated sugar
1/2 cup water
1 1/2 teaspoons clear vanilla (dark vanilla can be used if clear is not available)

Line an 8-inch square pan with foil, and butter it generously. Set aside. Have everything measured and ready before starting. Chop the chocolate into 1-inch pieces. Put egg whites into a mixing bowl within reach, ready to turn mixer on.

Place corn syrup, sugar and water in a heavy 4-quart saucepan over medium heat. Stir constantly with a wooden spoon. Place a candy thermometer into the saucepan and heat to 225 degrees. When mixture reaches 225 degrees, turn mixer on and beat the egg whites until stiff. When mixture reaches 240 degrees, use a metal measuring cup and remove 3/4 cup of the hot mixture. Slowly pour it into the egg whites, while mixing on lowest speed. Continue mixing on low while you cook the remaining sugar mixture to 275 degrees.

Turn mixer to medium, and slowly and in a thin stream, add the rest of the syrup. When mixed thoroughly, turn mixer off. Using a wooden spoon, stir in chocolate and vanilla until chocolate is melted.

Pour into the prepared pan. Allow to set up overnight at room temperature, or in refrigerator for faster set time.

When set, cut into bars or squares.

Store wrapped in plastic wrap.

Yield: 64 1-inch pieces

Chocolate Nougat

Chocolate lovers give this nougat high marks. I bet you will, too.

8 ounces milk- or dark chocolate
3 large egg whites, at room temperature
2 3/4 cups light corn syrup
1 1/3 cups granulated sugar
1/2 cup water
1 1/2 teaspoons vanilla (use clear vanilla if available)

Line an 8-inch square pan with foil and butter the foil generously. Set aside. Measure all ingredients before starting. Place the egg whites in a mixing bowl, and set aside, ready to beat. Chop the chocolate into 1-inch pieces.

Put the corn syrup, sugar and water into a heavy 3-quart saucepan. Heat, stirring constantly with a wooden spoon. Place a candy thermometer into the saucepan. When mixture reaches 225 degrees, turn on the mixer and beat the egg whites until stiff, but not dry, as the syrup mixture continues to cook. Continue to heat mixture until it reaches 240 degrees. Slowly pour 3/4 of a cup of the hot mixture into the beaten egg whites, beating constantly on low. Continue beating slowly while heating the remaining syrup to 275 degrees.

Turn heat to medium under egg white mixture and, in a thin stream, slowly add the remaining syrup into the egg white mixture until well blended. Turn off the mixer and remove blade. With a wooden spoon, stir in the chopped chocolate and vanilla until the chocolate is melted.

Pour into the prepared pan and set up at room temperature. For a quicker cooling time, mixture can be placed in refrigerator. When cool, cut into bars or squares.

Store, wrapped in plastic wrap.

Yield: 64 1-inch pieces

Honey Nut Nougats

How do you make a nutty nougat even more delicious? Dip it in chocolate.

1 cup nuts, such as walnuts
1 cup granulated sugar
1/2 cup honey
1/3 cup light corn syrup
1/4 cup water
2 1/3 cups marshmallow creme
1 1/2 tablespoons vegetable shortening
6 tablespoons confectioners sugar
1 pound milk- or dark chocolate for dipping

Line an 8-inch square pan with foil and butter the foil generously. Set aside.

Finely chop the nuts. Set aside.

Place the sugar, honey, corn syrup and water into a heavy 4-quart saucepan. Place a candy thermometer into the saucepan and heat to 272 degrees.

Remove from the heat and let rest for 10 minutes. Add the marshmallow creme and shortening. Beat by hand or with a mixer until well blended. Fold in the confectioners' sugar and the chopped nuts.

Pour into the prepared pan. Set up at room temperature for 24 hours.

When set, chop the chocolate into 1-inch pieces. Fill the bottom of a double boiler with very hot tap water. Put the chopped chocolate in the top of the double boiler and place over bottom of double boiler. Stir until chocolate is melted.

Cut chilled mixture into 1-inch squares. Using a dipping fork or dipping spoon, dip nougats into the melted chocolate. Place on parchment paper.

Store in an airtight container.

Yield: 64 nougats

Nougat Caramel Pinwheels

Make the special people in your life happy today with nougat caramel pinwheels.

3/4 cup butter
2 cups brown sugar, firmly packed
Pinch of salt
3/4 cup light corn syrup
1 14-ounce can sweetened condensed milk
1/2 teaspoon vanilla

Line a 9- X 13-inch pan with foil and butter it generously. Set aside.

In a heavy 4-quart saucepan, melt the butter over medium heat. Using a wooden spoon, stir in sugar, salt and corn syrup until dissolved. Then, add the sweetened condensed milk. Place a candy thermometer into the saucepan and, stirring constantly, heat to 243 degrees.

Remove from heat. Stir in vanilla. Pour into prepared pan. Allow to set up at room temperature. Meanwhile, prepare the nougat.

VANILLA NOUGAT

8 ounces white chocolate
3 large egg whites, at room temperature
2 3/4 cups light corn syrup
1 1/3 cups granulated sugar
1/2 cup water
1 1/2 teaspoons clear vanilla (dark vanilla can be used if clear
   is not available)

Have everything measured and ready before starting. Chop the chocolate into 1-inch pieces. Put egg whites into a mixing bowl within reach, ready to turn mixer on.

continued on following page ☞ ☞ ☞

74

Nougat Caramel Pinwheels *(continued)*

Place corn syrup, sugar and water in a heavy 4-quart saucepan over medium heat. Stir constantly with a wooden spoon. Place a candy thermometer into the saucepan and heat to 225 degrees. When 225 degrees is reached, turn mixer on and beat the egg whites until stiff. When mixture reaches 240 degrees, using a metal measuring cup, remove 3/4 cup of the hot mixture. Slowly pour it into the egg whites, while mixing on lowest speed. Continue mixing on low while you cook the remaining sugar mixture to 275 degrees.

Turn mixer to medium, and slowly and in a thin stream, add the rest of the syrup. When mixed thoroughly, turn mixer off and stir in chocolate and vanilla with a wooden spoon until chocolate is melted.

Pour mixture over the caramel, leaving about 2 inches at one long end uncovered. Press nougat onto caramel with buttered spatula or hands. Allow to set up at room temperature for several hours.

Remove the candy from the pan with buttered hands, and start rolling the cylinder up tightly, starting with the end covered with nougat. You can lengthen the cylinder by rolling it with your hands near the center and gently pressing and moving them toward the ends. The cylinder can be cut into 2 or 3 pieces to make it easier to work with.

When the cylinder is 2 inches in diameter, slice into 1/2-inch pieces using a sharp knife in a sawing motion.

Store in candy cups, wrapped in plastic wrap.

Yield: 55 pieces

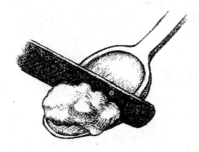

Peanut Nougat Log

White chocolate and roasted peanuts co-star in this sweet production.

8 ounces white chocolate
3 large egg whites, at room temperature
2 3/4 cups light corn syrup
1 1/3 cups granulated sugar
1/2 cup water
1 1/2 teaspoons clear vanilla (dark vanilla can be used if clear
  is not available)
2 cups chopped blanched roasted peanuts

Line a cookie sheet with foil, and butter it generously. Set aside. Have everything measured and ready before starting. Chop the chocolate into 1-inch pieces. Put egg whites into a mixing bowl within reach, ready to turn mixer on. Chop the peanuts.

Place corn syrup, sugar and water in a heavy 4-quart saucepan over medium heat. Stir constantly with a wooden spoon. Place a candy thermometer into the saucepan and heat to 225 degrees. When mixture reaches 225 degrees, turn mixer on and beat the egg whites until stiff. When mixture reaches 240 degrees, using a metal measuring cup, remove 3/4 cup of the hot mixture. Slowly pour it into the egg whites while mixing on lowest speed. Continue mixing on low while you cook the remaining sugar mixture to 275 degrees.

Turn mixer to medium, and slowly and in a thin stream, add the rest of the syrup. When mixed thoroughly, turn mixer off and stir in chocolate and vanilla with a wooden spoon until chocolate is melted.

Roll into logs, 3/4 X 1 1/2 inches, place on foil-lined cookie sheet, and place in freezer for 2 hours or until frozen. Meanwhile, prepare caramel as follows.

continued on following page ☞ ☞ ☞

Peanut and Nougat Log *(continued)*

　　3/4 cup butter
　　2 cups brown sugar, firmly packed
　　Pinch of salt
　　3/4 cup light corn syrup
　　1 14-ounce can sweetened condensed milk
　　1/2 teaspoon vanilla

Line a 9-inch square pan with foil and butter it generously. Set aside.

In a heavy 4-quart saucepan, melt the butter over medium heat. Using a wooden spoon, stir in sugar, salt and corn syrup until dissolved. Then, add the sweetened condensed milk. Place a candy thermometer into the saucepan and, stirring constantly, heat to 243 degrees.

Remove from heat. Stir in vanilla. Pour into top of double boiler and place over bottom, which has been filled with very hot tap water.

Drop frozen nougat logs into melted caramel one at a time, and remove with a dipping fork. Roll logs into peanuts to cover. Return to prepared cookie sheet to set up.

Store wrapped in plastic wrap.

Yield: 30 bars

NUTS,
CLUSTERS
& CHEWS

Glazed Nuts

Small dishes of glazed nuts are perfectly delightful for light nibbling.

4 cups mixed nuts (without peanuts) or 4 cups walnut halves
2 cups granulated sugar
1/2 cup water
1 cup light corn syrup
2 teaspoons liquid butter flavoring
1 teaspoon vanilla

Place the nuts on a cookie sheet and bake in a 350 degree oven for 4 to 5 minutes.

Generously butter a cookie sheet or jelly roll pan. Set aside.

Place the sugar, water and syrup in a heavy 3-quart saucepan. Bring to a boil. Place a candy thermometer into the saucepan and heat to 290 degrees, stirring occasionally.

Remove from heat and stir in the butter flavor and vanilla. Add the warm nuts. Stir until nuts are well coated.

Pour out onto the prepared cookie sheet, and spread as thin as possible. Set up at room temperature. When cool, break into bite-size pieces.

If desired, pieces can be dipped in melted chocolate.

Store in an airtight container.

Yield: 4 cups

Almond Clusters

Almonds are native to Asia and northern Africa, but also thrive in other parts of the world, including the U.S.A. Almond trees are exquisite when in bloom, and of course, their nuts are delicious.

    1 pound dark chocolate
    1 tablespoon vegetable oil
    1 pound almonds

Line two cookie sheets with parchment paper. Set aside.

Roast the nuts in a 9- X 13-inch cake pan in a 325 degree oven for 10 minutes. Cool to room temperature.

Chop the chocolate into 1-inch pieces. Fill the bottom of a double boiler with very hot tap water. Put the chopped chocolate and vegetable oil in the top pan and place over bottom. Stir until chocolate is melted and vegetable oil is incorporated.

Add the roasted nuts to the melted chocolate. Stir well to coat, and drop by teaspoonful onto the prepared cookie sheets. Set up at room temperature.

Store in a covered container.

Yield: 70 bite-size clusters

Macadamia Nut Clusters

Some people are adamant: "Make it with macadamias or don't make it at all!"

        1 pound milk- or dark chocolate
        2 teaspoons vegetable oil
        1 pound macadamia nuts

Line two cookie sheets with parchment paper. Set aside.

Roast the nuts in a 9- X 13-inch cake pan in a 325 degree oven for 5 to 8 minutes. Let cool to room temperature.

Chop the chocolate into 1-inch pieces. Fill the bottom of a double boiler with very hot tap water. Put the chopped chocolate and vegetable oil in the top pan and place over bottom. Stir until chocolate is melted and oil is incorporated.

Add the roasted nuts to the melted chocolate. Stir well to coat, and drop by teaspoonful onto the prepared cookie sheets. Set up at room temperature.

Store in a covered container.

Yield: 65 clusters

Peanut Clusters

Dry roasted peanuts work very well in this taste-tempting classic.

      1 pound milk- or dark chocolate
      1 pound roasted peanuts (or dry roasted)
      1 tablespoon vegetable oil

Chop the chocolate into 1-inch pieces. Fill the bottom of a double boiler with very hot tap water. Put the chopped chocolate in the top of the double boiler and place over bottom of double boiler. Stir until chocolate is melted. Add the oil and stir well. The oil prevents the chocolate from setting up and becoming too firm.

Add the peanuts, stirring to coat. Drop by teaspoonful onto parchment paper. Set up at room temperature.

Store in a covered container.

Yield: 85 clusters

Raisin Clusters

I heard it through the grapevine, raisin clusters are a hit!

1 pound milk- or dark chocolate
2 teaspoons vegetable oil
1 pound raisins

Line two cookie sheets with parchment paper. Set aside.

Chop the chocolate into 1-inch pieces.

Fill the bottom of a double boiler with very hot tap water. Put the chopped chocolate and vegetable oil in the top pan, and place over bottom. Stir until chocolate is melted and vegetable oil is incorporated.

Add the raisins to the chocolate. Stir well to coat.

Drop by teaspoonful onto the prepared cookie sheet. Set up at room temperature.

Store in a covered container.

Yield: 75 clusters

Turtles

These turtles have chocolate "shells" and pecan "heads" and "feet."

3/4 cup pecans
2 cups heavy cream
1 3/4 cups granulated sugar
1/4 cup light brown sugar
1 cup light corn syrup
1/4 cup butter
1/4 teaspoon salt
1 teaspoon vanilla
1 pound milk chocolate
2 teaspoons vegetable oil
192 pecan halves (3/4 of a pound)

Measure all ingredients before you begin. Finely chop 3/4 cup of the pecans. Line an 8-inch square pan with foil and butter it generously. Set aside.

Using a small saucepan, heat the heavy cream until warm.

Remove 1 cup of the warm cream, and place it into a heavy 4-quart saucepan. Add the sugar and corn syrup to the cream in the 4-quart saucepan. Heat on medium for about 5 minutes, stirring with a wooden spoon, until mixture begins to boil. Add the remaining cream very slowly, so the boiling does not stop. Cook about 5 minutes more.

Place a candy thermometer into the saucepan and heat to 230 degrees. Lower the heat to prevent scorching. Add the butter slowly, and heat to 245 degrees.

Remove the candy from the heat, and stir in the salt, vanilla and chopped pecans. Pour mixture into the prepared pan. Set up at room temperature until firm, or overnight. Cut into 1-inch squares.

continued on following page ☞ ☞ ☞

Turtles (*continued)*

While caramel is setting up, chop the milk chocolate into 1-inch pieces. Fill the bottom of a double boiler with very hot tap water. Put the chopped chocolate in the top of the double boiler and place over bottom of double boiler. Stir until chocolate is melted. Add the vegetable oil and stir well.

Arrange the pecan halves on parchment paper, to form a cross (the 4 inside pieces touching). Place a 1-inch flattened piece of caramel in the center of the pecans. Pour the melted chocolate over the caramel and let it drip down the sides to the parchment. Do not cover all of the pecans. Let the turtle set up at room temperature. When set, pick up each turtle and spoon a 1/2 teaspoon puddle of chocolate onto the parchment and set the turtle down into the chocolate puddle. Allow to set up at room temperature.

Store in an airtight container.

Yield: 48 turtles

Butterscotch Chews

Ingredients from your cereal cupboard make these chews crisp and crunchy.

12 ounces butterscotch chips
7 ounces sweetened condensed milk
1 cup Grapenuts™ cereal
1 cup crisp rice cereal
3/4 cup golden raisins

Line a cookie sheet with parchment paper. Set aside.

Fill the bottom of a double boiler with very hot tap water. Put the chips and sweetened condensed milk in the top of the double boiler and place over bottom of double boiler. Stir until mixture begins to thicken and is smooth.

Remove top of double boiler from the bottom, and add the cereal and raisins to the hot mixture. Stir until coated.

Drop by teaspoonful onto the prepared cookie sheet. Chill for 2 to 3 hours.

Store in a covered container in a cool place.

Yield: 45 chews

Tangy Apricot Chews

The combination of fruits, nuts, and white chocolate is excellent.

1 pound white chocolate
2 tablespoons butter
3/4 cup chopped dried apricots
1/2 cup Grapenuts cereal
1/2 cup pecans, chopped
1/2 cup raisins
1/2 cup coconut

Chop the white chocolate into 1-inch pieces. Fill the bottom of a double boiler with very hot tap water. Put the chopped white chocolate in the top of the double boiler and place over bottom of double boiler. Stir until chocolate is melted.

Remove top of double boiler from bottom. Add remaining ingredients to chocolate, and stir until well coated. Drop by teaspoonful onto parchment paper. Set up at room temperature or in the refrigerator.

Store in an airtight container.

Yield: 45 chews

Cashew Crunch

Pretzel sticks in candy? You bet! And I bet you'll love it.

    1 pound white chocolate
    1 tablespoon vegetable oil
    1/3 pound cashews
    1 1/4 cups pretzel sticks

Line two cookie sheets with parchment paper. Set aside.

Roast the cashews in a 9- X 13-inch cake pan in a 325 degree oven for about 8 minutes. Cool, and chop coarsely.

Break the pretzel sticks into 1-inch long pieces.

Chop the chocolate into 1-inch pieces. Fill the bottom of a double boiler with very hot tap water. Put the chopped chocolate and vegetable oil in the top pan and place over bottom. Stir until chocolate is melted and vegetable oil in incorporated.

Stir the nuts and pretzels into the melted chocolate, and drop by teaspoonful onto the prepared cookie sheets. Allow to set up at room temperature.

Store in a covered container.

Yield: 50 bite-size pieces

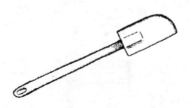

Candy Hash

White chocolate hash is delicious and delightful.

1 pound white chocolate
1/3 cup sliced almonds
3/4 cup dry roasted peanuts
1 1/4 cups fruity "O" cereal
1/2 cup crisp rice cereal
1 cup miniature marshmallows

Line a cookie sheet with parchment paper and set aside.

Chop the chocolate into 1-inch pieces. Fill the bottom of a double boiler with very hot tap water. Put the chopped chocolate in the top of the double boiler and place over bottom of double boiler. Stir until chocolate is melted.

Place the sliced almonds in a pie tin and toast in a 325 degree oven for about 5 minutes or until lightly browned. Cool.

Mix the toasted almonds, peanuts, cereals and marshmallows in a large bowl. Pour the melted chocolate over the mixture and stir until well mixed.

Drop by teaspoonful onto the prepared cookie sheet. Allow to set up at room temperature, 10 to 15 minutes.

Store in an airtight container.

Yield: 50 pieces

Pralines

"I first tasted pralines while vacationing in the southern part of the United States. Later, I was delighted to discover this wonderful confection was also available up North."

Sweet Memories

2/3 cup lightly-packed light brown sugar
2/3 cup granulated sugar
1/2 cup whipping cream
1/2 teaspoon vanilla
6 ounces pecan halves

Lightly butter a cookie sheet, and set aside.

Roast the pecans on a cookie sheet in a 325 degree oven for 10 minutes.

Place the brown and granulated sugars and the cream in a heavy 3-quart saucepan. Cook over medium heat, stirring with a wooden spoon, until the sugar is dissolved, about 5 minutes. Place a candy thermometer in the pan and lower the heat to medium-low. Stir constantly, and cook to 236 degrees. Remove pan from heat, and stir in the vanilla and roasted pecan halves. Stir until the mixture is a little lighter in color, and the nuts are well coated.

Working quickly, drop by tablespoon onto the prepared cookie sheet. The patties should be 2 1/3 inches across. Cool at room temperature until firm.

Store, wrapping each piece in plastic wrap.

Yield: 20 pieces

CREAM
CENTERS

No-Cook Vanilla Butter Cream Center

No one will guess how quickly and easily you prepared this butter cream filling.

3 3/4 cups confectioners' sugar
1/4 cup light corn syrup
2 1/2 tablespoons water
1/4 teaspoon salt
1/2 teaspoon vanilla
1/3 cup butter
1 pound milk or dark chocolate for dipping

Line a cookie sheet with parchment paper and set aside.

Place half the confectioners' sugar in a large mixing bowl with the corn syrup, water, salt, vanilla and butter. Mix on low speed until blended. Slowly add the remaining confectioners' sugar, mixing on low until smooth, about 5 minutes.

Chill in refrigerator for 3 to 4 hours.

After mixture is chilled, chop the chocolate into 1-inch pieces. Fill the bottom of a double boiler with very hot tap water. Put the chopped chocolate in the top of the double boiler and place over bottom of double boiler. Stir until chocolate is melted.

Roll chilled mixture into 3/4-inch balls; place on prepared cookie sheet and chill for 5 to 8 minutes. Using a dipping fork or dipping spoon, dip rolled mixture into the melted chocolate, and place on parchment paper.

Store in an airtight container.

Yield: 30 centers

Quick and Easy Cream Center

Marshmallow cream and non-dairy coffee creamer team up in this no-cook cream center.

2 1/2 cups confectioners' sugar
3 tablespoons butter
1/2 cup marshmallow cream
1/2 cup light corn syrup
2 tablespoons liquid non-dairy coffee creamer
1 1/2 teaspoons vanilla
1 pound milk or dark chocolate for dipping

Line a cookie sheet with parchment paper and set aside.

Place the butter, marshmallow cream, light corn syrup, creamer and vanilla in a large mixing bowl. Mix slowly on low while adding the confectioners' sugar a little at a time. Increase mixer speed as the ingredients blend together. Mix for 3 to 5 minutes. Chill for 2 to 3 hours.

Roll chilled mixture into 3/4-inch balls. Place on prepared cookie sheet. Chill 5 to 8 minutes.

Meanwhile, chop the chocolate into 1-inch pieces. Fill the bottom of a double boiler with very hot tap water. Put the chopped chocolate in the top of the double boiler and place over bottom of double boiler. Stir until chocolate is melted. Using a dipping fork or dipping spoon, dip rolled mixture into the melted chocolate. Place back on prepared cookie sheet to set up at room temperature.

Store in a covered container.

Yield: 50 centers

Mix and Match Butter Cream Centers

Use a microwave to save time with this recipe. Select your favorite flavored chips for a personalized butter cream center.

> 2/3 cup semi-sweet chocolate chips, peanut butter chips, or
>   vanilla milk flavored chips
> 1/2 cup butter, softened
> 1/4 cup whipping cream
> 1 teaspoon vanilla extract
> 3 1/2 to 4 cups powdered sugar, divided

Line a cookie sheet with parchment paper; set aside.

In small microwave-safe bowl, place desired flavor of chips. Microwave at HIGH (100%) for 30 seconds to 1 minute, or until chips are melted when stirred.

In small mixing bowl, beat butter, whipping cream and vanilla until fluffy; gradually blend in 1 cup powdered sugar. Gradually stir in melted chips and remaining 2½ to 3 cups powdered sugar, stirring until mixture holds its shape. If necessary, cover and refrigerate until mixture can be shaped.

Shape mixture into 1-inch balls and place on prepared cookie sheet. Refrigerate until balls (centers) are firm and dry on surface, several hours or overnight. Coat with Simple Chocolate Coating, Peanut Butter, or Vanilla Chip Coating. (If centers are too cold, the coating may crack. If this happens, dip them again after they set up.)

Store in a covered container.

Yield: About 48 cream centers

Maple Creams

Candy as we know it today did not exist in Colonial America so folk satisfied their sweet tooth with maple syrup and maple sugar. Aren't you glad we don't have to tap a maple tree to enjoy that marvelous flavor today?

1 1/2 cups brown sugar
1/4 cup butter
1/4 cup water
1/2 cup heavy cream
1/2 cup marshmallow creme
1 teaspoon maple extract
1/2 cup confectioners' sugar
1 pound milk or dark chocolate for dipping

Before you begin, place a large mixing bowl and beaters in the freezer to chill. Line a cookie sheet with parchment paper; set aside.

Chop the chocolate into 1-inch pieces. Fill the bottom of a double boiler with very hot tap water. Put the chopped chocolate in the top of the double boiler and place over bottom of double boiler. Stir until chocolate is melted.

Place the brown sugar, butter and water in a heavy 2-quart saucepan. Place a candy thermometer into the saucepan and heat to 215 degrees. Very slowly, add the cream, so not to break the boiling. Heat to 240 degrees. Remove from heat.

Pour hot mixture into the chilled bowl, and let stand until mixture is lukewarm.

Beat mixture slowly, while adding the marshmallow creme and flavoring. Then, gradually, add the confectioners' sugar. An additional 1/4 cup sugar may be needed. Continue beating on medium for 5 minutes. Form into 3/4-inch balls. Place on prepared cookie sheet and chill for 5 to 8 minutes. Using a dipping fork or dipping spoon, dip rolled mixture into the melted chocolate, and place on parchment paper. Set up at room temperature.

Store in an airtight container.

Yield: 45 creams

Maple Nut Creams

If you prefer nuts in your maple cream, you'll love this recipe.

1 1/2 cups brown sugar
1/4 cup water
1/4 cup butter
1/2 cup heavy cream
1/2 cup marshmallow cream
3 teaspoons maple flavoring
1/2 cup nuts, such as walnuts
1/2 to 3/4 cup confectioners' sugar
1 pound milk or dark chocolate for dipping

Before you begin, place a large mixing bowl and beaters in the freezer to chill. Finely chop the nuts. Line a cookie sheet with parchment paper and set aside.

Place the brown sugar, water, marshmallow cream and butter in a heavy 3-quart saucepan. Place a candy thermometer into the saucepan and heat to 215 degrees, stirring with a wooden spoon. Add the heavy cream very slowly, so the boiling does not stop. Heat to 240 degrees.

Remove from heat and pour into the cold mixing bowl. Mix on low while slowly adding the confectioners' sugar and the nuts. Continue beating for 5 minutes. Cover and chill for 1 to 2 hours.

Chop the chocolate into 1-inch pieces. Fill the bottom of a double boiler with very hot tap water. Put the chopped chocolate in the top of the double boiler and place over bottom of double boiler. Stir until chocolate is melted.

Roll the chilled mixture into 3/4-inch balls and place on prepared cookie sheet. Chill for 5 to 8 minutes. Using a dipping fork or dipping spoon, dip rolled mixture into the melted chocolate, and return to parchment paper.

Store in an airtight container.

Yield: 45 creams

Bordeaux

Dark brown sugar and powdered instant coffee create a robust flavor.

1 1/2 cups dark brown sugar
1/4 cup butter
1 cup sour cream
2 cups confectioners' sugar
1 teaspoon powdered instant coffee
Pinch of salt
1 pound milk- or dark chocolate for dipping

Before you begin, place a large mixing bowl and beaters in the freezer to chill.

Place brown sugar, butter and sour cream in a heavy 2-quart saucepan. Bring to a boil, stirring constantly. Reduce the heat to low, and continue cooking for 2 minutes, stirring constantly. Stir in the coffee and salt. Continue boiling for 30 seconds.

Remove from heat and pour sugar mixture into the chilled mixing bowl. Let set 10 minutes. Then, slowly, add the confectioners' sugar while mixing on low. After all the sugar is incorporated, mix 5 minutes more. Roll into 3/4-inch balls, and chill for 8 to 10 minutes.

Meanwhile, chop the chocolate into 1-inch pieces. Fill the bottom of a double boiler with very hot tap water. Put the chopped chocolate in the top of the double boiler and place over bottom of double boiler. Stir until chocolate is melted.

Using a dipping fork or dipping spoon, dip rolled mixture into the melted chocolate. You may want to sprinkle chocolate shots on the top before they set up, to look like real Bordeaux. Set up at room temperature on parchment paper.

Store in an airtight container.

Yield: 55 Bordeaux

Butterscotch Creams

Combine packaged butterscotch chips and butterscotch flavoring for a richer butterscotch flavor.

1 1/2 cups butterscotch chips
2 3-ounce packages cream cheese
2 cups confectioners' sugar
1 teaspoon butterscotch flavoring
1 pound milk chocolate, dark chocolate or butterscotch chips
    for dipping

Line an 8-inch square pan with plastic wrap. Set aside. Line a cookie sheet with parchment paper; set aside.

Fill the bottom of a double boiler with very hot tap water. Put the 1 1/2 cups of butterscotch chips in the top of the double boiler and place over bottom of double boiler. Stir until chips are melted. Add the cream cheese and stir until blended.

Remove top of double boiler from bottom, and, to the butterscotch mixture, slowly stir in the confectioners' sugar. If desired, place in mixing bowl and slowly blend in confectioners' sugar with mixer. Pour into the prepared pan and chill overnight.

Roll chilled mixture into 3/4-inch balls and place on prepared cookie sheet. Chill for 8 to 10 minutes.

Meanwhile, if using chocolate, chop it into 1-inch pieces. Fill the bottom of a double boiler with very hot tap water. Put the chopped chocolate or butterscotch chips in the top of the double boiler and place over bottom of double boiler. Stir until melted. Using a dipping fork or dipping spoon, dip rolled mixture into the melted chocolate. Return to prepared cookie sheet to set up at room temperature.

Store in a covered container.

Yield: 40 creams

Creamy Chocolate Centers

Chocolate centers covered with chocolate. What more could a chocoholic ask for?

>   1 pound milk- or dark chocolate
>   3 tablespoons butter
>   1 14-ounce can sweetened condensed milk
>   1 pound milk- or dark chocolate for dipping

Line an 8-inch square pan with plastic wrap. Set aside.

Chop the 1 pound of milk chocolate into 1-inch pieces. Fill the bottom of a double boiler with very hot tap water. Put the chopped chocolate in the top of double boiler and place over the bottom. Stir until chocolate is melted.

To the melted chocolate, add the butter. Stir until butter is melted and well incorporated.

Remove double boiler top from bottom. To the chocolate-butter mixture, add the sweetened condensed milk, stirring until well blended.

Pour into the prepared pan and let cool at room temperature until set. Roll into 3/4-inch balls.

Meanwhile, chop the remaining pound of milk or dark chocolate. Fill the bottom of a double boiler with very hot tap water. Put the chopped chocolate in the top of the double boiler and place over bottom of double boiler. Stir until chocolate is melted.

Using a dipping fork or dipping spoon, dip rolled mixture into the melted chocolate. Place on parchment paper to set up.

Store in an airtight container.

Yield: 55 centers

Lemon Creams

Tangy, aromatic lemon creams are as refreshing as spring sunshine.

5 cups confectioners' sugar
1/4 cup softened butter
3/4 cup marshmallow cream
2 1/2 tablespoons lemon juice
1/4 teaspoon salt
1/2 teaspoon vanilla
1 teaspoon grated lemon rind
4 to 6 drops yellow food coloring (optional)
1 pound milk- or dark chocolate for dipping

Line a cookie sheet with parchment paper; set aside.

Chop the chocolate into 1-inch pieces. Fill the bottom of a double boiler with very hot tap water. Put the chopped chocolate in the top of the double boiler and place over bottom of double boiler. Stir until chocolate is melted.

Place 2 cups of the confectioners' sugar, along with the butter, marshmallow cream, lemon juice, salt, vanilla, lemon rind and, food coloring if desired, in a large mixing bowl. Mix until creamy and smooth.

Gradually add the remaining confectioners' sugar. Mix until well blended, or knead until smooth by hand on a cutting board which has been dusted with confectioners' sugar.

Roll into 3/4-inch balls and place on prepared cookie sheet. Chill for 5 to 8 minutes. Using a dipping fork or dipping spoon, dip rolled mixture into the melted chocolate, and place on parchment paper until set.

Store in an airtight container.

Yield: 45 pieces

Orange Cream Center

Using orange juice concentrate gives candy wonderful flavor and saves you time.

        3 1/2 cups granulated sugar
        3/4 cup orange juice concentrate
        1/3 cup heavy cream
        Pinch of salt
        3/4 cup butter
        1 1/2 pounds milk- or dark chocolate for dipping

Before you begin, place a large mixing bowl and beaters in the freezer to chill. Line a cookie sheet with parchment paper and set aside.

Put sugar, orange juice, heavy cream, salt and butter in a heavy 4-quart saucepan. Cook over medium-high heat. As the mixture begins to thicken, lower the heat to medium-low. Place a candy thermometer into the saucepan and, stirring occasionally, heat to 240 degrees. Remove from heat.

Pour mixture into the cold mixing bowl. Place in the refrigerator, stirring every 15 minutes, until mixture is lukewarm.

Beat on low for 5 to 10 minutes, and increase speed as it thickens. When thick enough to form a ball, cover and refrigerate for 3 to 4 hours.

Meanwhile, chop the chocolate into 1-inch pieces. Fill the bottom of a double boiler with very hot tap water. Put the chopped chocolate in the top of the double boiler and place over bottom of double boiler. Stir until chocolate is melted.

Roll chilled mixture into 3/4-inch balls and place on prepared cookie sheet. Chill for 8 to 10 minutes. Using a dipping fork or dipping spoon, dip rolled mixture into the melted chocolate. Return to prepared cookie sheet.

Store in an airtight container.

Yield: 70 centers

Chocolate Malted Creams

Creamy malt-flavored centers are dipped in chocolate for a real taste treat.

    1/2 cup whipping cream
    1 pound milk chocolate
    1/4 cup powdered malt
    1 pound milk chocolate for dipping

Line a cookie sheet with parchment paper and set aside. Chop 1 pound of the milk chocolate into 1-inch pieces.

Scald the cream by placing in a medium saucepan over medium heat, and bring just to the boiling point. Do not allow cream to boil.

Remove from heat and add the chopped chocolate, stirring to melt. Add the malt powder, and stir until smooth. Pour into a mixing bowl and chill 2 to 3 hours.

Whip chilled mixture at high speed with a heavy mixer until fluffy. Chill again until mixture is firm enough to handle. Roll into 1-inch balls and place on the prepared cookie sheet. Refrigerate for 8 to 10 minutes.

Meanwhile, chop the remaining pound of milk chocolate into 1-inch pieces. Fill the bottom of a double boiler with very hot tap water. Put the chopped chocolate in the top of the double boiler and place over bottom of double boiler. Stir until chocolate is melted.

Using a dipping fork or dipping spoon, dip rolled mixture into the melted chocolate, and place on parchment paper. Set up at room temperature.

Store in a covered container.

Yield: 40 creams

Brown and White Balls

Double your flavor and your fun with candies that are half chocolate, half vanilla.

3/4 pound dark chocolate
3 tablespoons butter
10 1/2 ounces sweetened condensed milk
1/2 cup chocolate shots or sprinkles
1 egg white
3 tablespoons whipping cream, chilled
1/2 teaspoon vanilla
4 1/2 cups confectioners' sugar
1/2 cup additional confectioners' sugar for kneading
1/2 cup white shots or sprinkles

Line 2 cookie sheets with parchment paper and set aside. Measure the whipping cream and chill.

Chop the chocolate into 1-inch pieces. Fill the bottom of a double boiler with very hot tap water. Put the chopped chocolate in the top of the double boiler and place over bottom of double boiler. Stir until chocolate is melted. When melted, remove from heat and stir in the sweetened condensed milk. Blend well. Allow to cool until mixture can be rolled, approximately 30 minutes in refrigerator. Form chocolate mixture into 1 1/2-inch balls, then roll in the chocolate shots and place on prepared cookie sheet. Chill for 1 hour.

Meanwhile, beat the egg white, chilled whipping cream and vanilla. When well blended, slowly add the confectioners' sugar. Place mixture onto a cutting board which has been dusted with the 1/2 cup additional confectioners' sugar. Knead until smooth. Cover with plastic wrap and a damp cloth, and let stand for 1 hour. When firm, roll into 1 1/2-inch balls, then roll in the white shots and place on prepared cookie sheet. Chill for 1 hour.

Cut white and chocolate balls into quarters. Alternate the dark and white quarters to form new balls, each having two white and two chocolate sections. Chill.

Store in an airtight container.

Yield: 50 balls

Cinnamon Coffee Squares

This is a perfect candy to serve with espresso on a brisk fall day.

1/2 cup water
2 tablespoons dry instant coffee
2 1/2 cups granulated sugar
2 1/2 tablespoons heavy cream
2 tablespoons butter
Pinch of salt
1 1/2 teaspoons cinnamon
1 pound milk- or dark chocolate for dipping

Before you begin, place a large mixing bowl and beaters in the freezer to chill. Line an 8-inch square pan with plastic wrap and a cookie sheet with parchment paper. Set both aside.

Place the water and coffee in a heavy 3-quart saucepan, and bring to a boil stirring constantly. Reduce heat to medium and stir in sugar, heavy cream, butter, salt and cinnamon. When the sugar is dissolved, place candy thermometer into the saucepan and heat to 235 degrees. Remove from heat, and allow to cool to 115 degrees. Do not stir while cooling.

Remove bowl and beaters from freezer. Pour mixture into bowl and beat on medium to medium high, until candy begins to loose its shine, approximately 3 to 4 minutes. Pour into the prepared pan. Allow to set up at room temperature for 2 to 3 hours.

Meanwhile, chop the chocolate into 1-inch pieces. Fill the bottom of a double boiler with very hot tap water. Put the chopped chocolate in the top of the double boiler and place over bottom of double boiler. Stir until chocolate is melted.

Cut chilled mixture into 1-inch squares. Using a dipping fork or dipping spoon, dip rolled mixture into the melted chocolate. Place on prepared cookie sheet to set up.

Store in an airtight container.

Yield: 45 pieces

FRUIT & NUT CENTERS

Coconut Bon Bons

Coconut, marshmallows and dark chocolate make these bon bons fabulous.

1/2 cup light corn syrup
12 large marshmallows, cut into pieces
2 cups macaroon coconut
1 teaspoon vanilla
1 pound milk or dark chocolate for dipping

Line a cookie sheet with parchment paper; set aside.

Place the corn syrup and marshmallows in a heavy 3-quart saucepan. Cook, stirring with a wooden spoon, over medium heat until marshmallows are melted. Remove from the heat. Stir in the coconut and vanilla. Allow to cool at room temperature for 15 minutes.

Meanwhile, chop the chocolate into 1-inch pieces. Fill the bottom of a double boiler with very hot tap water. Put the chopped chocolate in the top of the double boiler and place over bottom of double boiler. Stir until chocolate is melted.

Roll chilled mixture into 3/4-inch balls. Using a dipping fork or dipping spoon, dip rolled mixture into the melted chocolate. Place on prepared cookie sheet to set up.

Store in an airtight container.

Yield: 40 pieces

Coconut Candy Bar Center

Rich coconut balls dipped in milk- or dark chocolate delight one and all.

    1 14-ounce can sweetened condensed milk
    8 ounces macaroon coconut
    1 teaspoon vanilla
    1/2 cup light corn syrup
    1 pound confectioners' sugar
    1 1/2 pounds milk or dark chocolate for dipping

Line a cookie sheet with parchment paper; set aside.

Place sweetened condensed milk, coconut, vanilla and corn syrup into a large mixing bowl. Mix on low until incorporated. Gradually add the confectioners' sugar and mix on low speed for 2 to 3 minutes. Store in the refrigerator until chilled.

Meanwhile, chop the chocolate into 1-inch pieces. Fill the bottom of a double boiler with very hot tap water. Put the chopped chocolate in the top of the double boiler and place over bottom of double boiler. Stir until chocolate is melted.

Roll chilled mixture into 3/4-inch balls and place on prepared cookie sheet. Using a dipping fork or dipping spoon, dip rolled mixture into the melted chocolate. Return to cookie sheet to set up.

Store in an airtight container.

Yield: 80 pieces

Coconut Kisses

These sweet, chocolate dipped kisses bring happy smiles to all.

2 tablespoons water
2 pounds confectioners' sugar
2 cups marshmallow cream
1 tablespoon butter
1/2 teaspoon glycerin (available at drug stores, or cake and
  candy supply stores)
3 1/2 cups flake coconut
1/4 teaspoon salt
3/4 teaspoon vanilla
1 pound milk or dark chocolate for dipping

Line a cookie sheet with parchment paper; set aside.

Stir the water, confectioners' sugar, marshmallow cream and butter together in a heavy 4-quart saucepan until well mixed. Place over very low heat. Place a candy thermometer into the saucepan and heat to 124 degrees, stirring often. Add the glycerin, coconut, salt and vanilla. Stir to mix well. Remove from the heat and let set 10 minutes.

Roll into 1-inch balls and shape into a cone. Place on the prepared cookie sheet. Allow to set up at room temperature.

Meanwhile, chop the chocolate into 1-inch pieces. Fill the bottom of a double boiler with very hot tap water. Put the chopped chocolate in the top of the double boiler and place over bottom of double boiler. Stir until chocolate is melted.

When firm, dip half of the cone, starting with the large end, into the melted chocolate. Return to prepared cookie sheet and allow to set up.

Store in an airtight container.

Yield: 55 kisses

Crunchy Date Nut Balls

Dates, nuts, and chocolate combine in this crispy, crunchy candy.

1/3 cup butter
3 cups miniature marshmallows
3 tablespoons half and half
2 cups crisp rice cereal
1 8-ounce package chopped dates
2 cups mini chocolate chips
3/4 cup finely chopped walnuts
1 cup confectioners' sugar, for dusting hands
1 1/2 pounds milk or dark chocolate for dipping

Line a cookie sheet with parchment paper; set aside.

Chop nuts finely; set aside.

Place the butter in a 4-quart saucepan, and melt over low heat. Add marshmallows and the half and half, stirring constantly until mixture is melted and smooth. Remove from heat and allow to cool until mixture thickens, 10 to 15 minutes.

Add rice cereal, dates, chocolate chips and nuts.

Dust hands well with confectioners' sugar and roll mixture into 1-inch balls. Chill in refrigerator for 8 to 10 minutes.

Meanwhile, chop the chocolate into 1-inch pieces. Fill the bottom of a double boiler with very hot tap water. Put the chopped chocolate in the top of the double boiler and place over bottom of double boiler. Stir until chocolate is melted. Using a dipping fork or dipping spoon, dip rolled mixture into the melted chocolate, and place on prepared cookie sheet. Allow to set up.

Store in an airtight container in the refrigerator.

Yield: 55 pieces

Fruit and Nut Center

This candy center features candied cherries, chopped nuts, and marshmallow cream. When dipped in chocolate, it's exquisite.

1/3 cup butter
2 cups granulated sugar
3/4 cup light corn syrup
1/2 cup hot water
7 ounces marshmallow cream
1 cup confectioners' sugar
1 1/2 cups candied cherries
1 cup chopped nuts, such as walnuts or pecans
1 pound milk or dark chocolate for dipping

Line a cookie sheet with parchment paper; set aside.

Melt the butter and allow to cool to room temperature.

Place the sugar, syrup and water in a heavy 3-quart saucepan. Cook over medium heat. Place a candy thermometer into the saucepan and heat to 265 degrees, stirring constantly with a wooden spoon. Remove from heat, add the marshmallow cream, and beat until almost firm. Pour mixture into a heavy mixing bowl and mix with a paddle. Add the melted butter, confectioners' sugar, candied fruit and nuts. Mix on medium until well mixed. Cover and chill for 2 to 3 hours, or overnight.

Meanwhile, chop the chocolate into 1-inch pieces. Fill the bottom of a double boiler with very hot tap water. Put the chopped chocolate in the top of the double boiler and place over bottom of double boiler. Stir until chocolate is melted.

Roll chilled mixture into 3/4-inch balls and place on prepared cookie sheet. Using a dipping fork or dipping spoon, dip rolled mixture into the melted chocolate. Return to cookie sheet to set up.

Store in an airtight container.

Yield: 55 centers

No-Cook Cherry Nut Centers

Quick and easy, this no-cook center is excellent when dipped in chocolate.

4 to 5 cups confectioners' sugar
1 tablespoon powdered egg white
2 to 3 tablespoons water
3 tablespoons cherry preserves
1 teaspoon cherry flavor (or candy oil to taste)
1/2 teaspoon citric acid
1/2 teaspoon vanilla
1/2 teaspoon liquid butter flavor
1/2 cup nuts, such as walnuts
1 1/2 pounds milk or dark chocolate for dipping

Line a cookie sheet with parchment paper; set aside.

Place half the confectioners' sugar and the remaining ingredients, except the dipping chocolate, in a large mixing bowl. Mix on low until incorporated, then turn on high for 5 minutes.

Turn mixer off, and add the remaining confectioners' sugar. Mix on low until mixture is uniform and smooth. Chill for 2 to 3 hours.

When the fruit-nut center is chilled, chop the chocolate into 1-inch pieces. Fill the bottom of a double boiler with very hot tap water. Put the chopped chocolate in the top of the double boiler and place over bottom of double boiler. Stir until chocolate is melted.

Roll chilled mixture into 3/4-inch balls. Using a dipping fork or dipping spoon, dip rolled mixture into the melted chocolate, and place on prepared cookie sheet.

Store in a covered container.

Yield: 45 centers.

Peanut Butter Balls

Enjoy that all-American favorite, peanut butter, enveloped with rich chocolate.

    1 1/2 cups peanut butter
    1/2 cup butter
    1 pound confectioners sugar
    1 teaspoon vanilla
    1 1/2 pounds milk or dark chocolate for dipping

Line a cookie sheet with parchment paper; set aside.

Chop the chocolate into 1-inch pieces. Fill the bottom of a double boiler with very hot tap water. Put the chopped chocolate in the top of the double boiler and place over bottom of double boiler. Stir until chocolate is melted. Set aside.

Place peanut butter, butter, sugar and vanilla in a large mixing bowl. Mix on low until creamy. Roll into 3/4-inch balls. Place on prepared cookie sheet, and chill for 5 to 8 minutes.

Using a dipping fork or dipping spoon, dip rolled mixture into the melted chocolate. Return to prepared cookie sheet to set up.

Store in a covered container.

Yield: 80 pieces

Crunchy Peanut Butter Centers

Crisp rice cereal and chunky peanut butter give this chocolate-dipped candy extra crunch.

2 cups crunchy peanut butter
1 cup butter, at room temperature
1 pound confectioners' sugar
2 1/2 cups crisp rice cereal
1 pound milk or dark chocolate for dipping

Line a cookie sheet with parchment paper; set aside.

Place the crunchy peanut butter and butter in a large mixing bowl. Mix on low until blended, then slowly add the confectioners' sugar. When mixed well, add the crisp rice cereal. Chill for 2 to 3 hours.

Chop the chocolate into 1-inch pieces. Fill the bottom of a double boiler with very hot tap water. Put the chopped chocolate in the top of the double boiler and place over bottom of double boiler. Stir until chocolate is melted.

Roll chilled mixture into 3/4-inch balls. Using a dipping fork or dipping spoon, dip rolled mixture into the melted chocolate, and place on prepared cookie sheet to set up.

Store in covered container.

Yield: 65 centers

Shirley's Chocolate Covered Cherries

Chocolate covered cherries are surprisingly easy to make. Try some soon.

2 pounds dark chocolate
60 maraschino cherries (2 10-ounce jars)
1 pound confectioners' sugar
1/2 cup butter, softened
1/2 cup sweetened condensed milk
1 teaspoon vanilla
1/2 cup additional confectioners' sugar for dusting hands

Line a cookie sheet with parchment paper; set aside.

Drain cherries on a paper towel.

Place the confectioners' sugar, softened butter, sweetened condensed milk and vanilla in a large mixing bowl, and mix until incorporated. Dust your hands with confectioners' sugar and shape the sugar-butter mixture around the well drained cherries. Place the cherries on the prepared cookie sheet. When all the cherries have been covered, place the cookie sheet into the freezer for 5 minutes to chill.

While cherries are chilling, chop chocolate into 1-inch pieces. Fill the bottom of a double boiler with very hot tap water. Put the chopped chocolate in the top of the double boiler and place over bottom of double boiler. Stir until chocolate is melted.

Remove the cherries from the freezer, and using a dipping fork or dipping spoon, dip cherries into the melted chocolate. Return to prepared cookie sheet.

For a liqueur taste, cherries can be soaked in brandy or your favorite liqueur for a few days prior to use.

Store in an airtight container.

Yield: 60 cherries

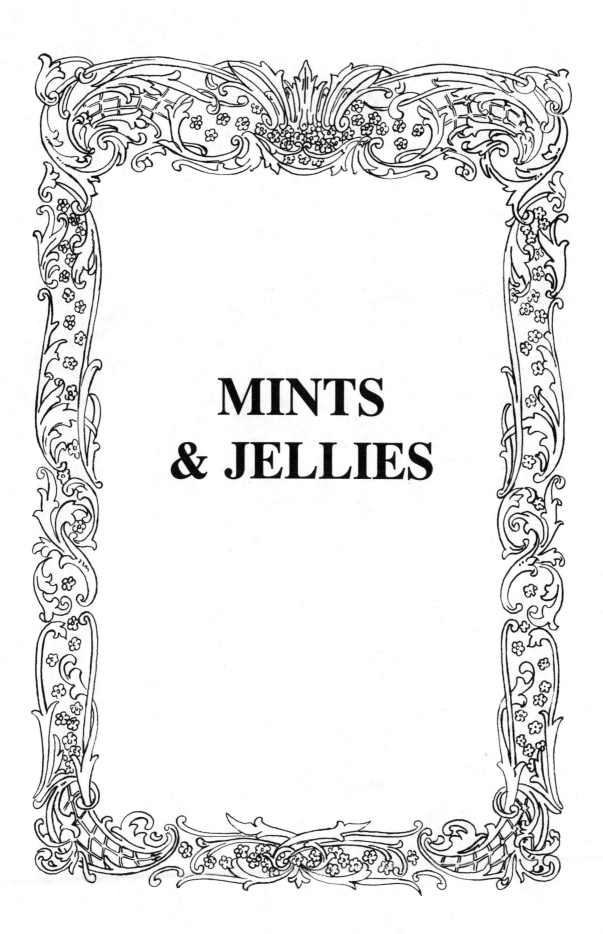

MINTS
& JELLIES

Butter Mints

Packaged white frosting mix makes these delicious buttery mints easy to make.

4 tablespoons butter
2 1/2 tablespoons whipping cream
1 14 1/2-ounce package creamy white frosting mix
1/8 teaspoon peppermint oil
Food coloring (such as green)

Line a cookie sheet with parchment paper and set aside.

Place the butter and whipping cream in a heavy 2-quart saucepan. Stir until butter is melted. Add the frosting mix, place a candy thermometer into the saucepan and heat to 150 degrees; do not overheat. Remove from heat and stir in the peppermint oil and food color.

Using a teaspoon, scoop out 1 teaspoon and roll into a ball. Place on the prepared cookie sheet. Flatten the ball into a patty about the size of a quarter. Set up at room temperature until firm.

Store in an airtight container in the refrigerator. Use within a few days.

Yield: 35 mints

Chocolate Mint Patties

"My grandma made the most fantastic peppermint patties! She arranged them on a beautiful china plate that had belonged to her mother, from whom she had been given the candy recipe, and served them with tea."
— *Sweet Memories*

3 2/3 cups (1 pound) powdered sugar
1/4 cup cocoa
1/3 cup butter or margarine, softened
1/3 cup light corn syrup
1 teaspoon peppermint extract

Line cookie sheet with parchment paper; set aside.

Sift together powdered sugar and cocoa; set aside.

In large mixing bowl, combine butter, corn syrup and peppermint extract. Mix on medium speed until well blended.

Gradually add 1 to 2 cups cocoa mixture, beating until well blended. With wooden spoon, stir in remaining cocoa mixture. With hands, knead until well blended and smooth.

Pat or roll to 1/4-inch thickness on wax paper. With small cookie cutters, cut into desired shapes. Or, using about 1 teaspoonful of chocolate mixture for each, shape into balls, then flatten into patties. Place on prepared cookie sheet. Let set up at room temperature until firm.

Store in airtight container in refrigerator.

Yield: About 7 dozen patties

Cream Cheese Mints

Shape this creamy mint into a ball, flatten it like a patty, or press it into a mold.

       2 3-ounce packages cream cheese, at room temperature
       Food color, as desired (red, green, etc.)
       Flavoring, as desired (peppermint, spearmint or wintergreen)
       4 1/2 cups confectioners' sugar
       3/4 cup super-fine sugar, in which to roll the mints
       1/2 cup confectioners' sugar, for kneading

Line cookie sheet with parchment paper and set aside.

Place the cream cheese in a large mixing bowl and beat until softened. Gradually and slowly, beat in the 4 1/2 cups confectioners' sugar. Knead the mixture on a cutting board which has been dusted with the additional 1/2 cup confectioners' sugar. Divide the mixture, and add the color and flavoring as desired.

Pinch off a small piece and form into a marble-size ball. Roll in the super-fine sugar. You can leave the mint in a round ball shape, or flatten like a patty. Or, press into either a soft rubber mold or clear plastic chocolate mold if shape is desired. Place on prepared cookie sheet.

Set up at room temperature for 2 to 3 hours.

Store in an airtight container in the refrigerator.

Yield: 80 bite-size pieces

Melt-in-Your-Mouth Mints

Classic chocolate-dipped mints are easy to make and always a hit.

1 pound milk- or dark chocolate
1/2 cup butter
1/8 teaspoon peppermint oil
1 pound milk- or dark chocolate for dipping

Line a cookie sheet with parchment paper, and line an 8-inch square pan with plastic wrap. Set both aside.

Chop the 1 pound chocolate into 1-inch pieces. Fill the bottom of a double boiler with very hot tap water. Put the chopped chocolate and butter in the top of the double boiler and place over bottom of double boiler. Stir until chocolate is melted and well mixed. Pour into a medium mixing bowl, and chill, stirring occasionally to keep the sides from setting up too hard. When mixture reaches the consistency of soft pudding, add the peppermint oil and beat with an electric mixer until light and fluffy, about 1 minute.

Pour into the lined pan. Place a piece of plastic wrap on top and press down gently to level the top. Allow to cool until firm, but not hard. Cut into 1-inch squares.

While mixture is cooling, melt the second pound of chocolate as described above. Using a dipping fork or dipping spoon, dip rolled mixture into the melted chocolate, and place on prepared cookie sheet to set up.

Store in an airtight container.

Yield: 64 pieces

Peppermint Patties

Sweetened condensed milk is a key ingredient in these chocolate dipped mints.

1 14-ounce can sweetened condensed milk
1 1/2 teaspoons peppermint extract
2 drops red or green food color (optional)
1/4 cup butter, at room temperature
5 to 6 cups confectioners' sugar
1 1/2 pounds milk- or dark chocolate for dipping

Line a cookie sheet with parchment paper and set aside.

Place the sweetened condensed milk, peppermint extract, butter and food color in a large mixing bowl. Beat on medium until well blended. Gradually add the confectioners' sugar until well blended.

Form into 1-inch balls and place on the prepared cookie sheet. Flatten each ball into a 2-inch patty. Chill for 8 to 10 minutes.

Meanwhile, chop the chocolate into 1-inch pieces. Fill the bottom of a double boiler with very hot tap water. Put the chopped chocolate in the top of the double boiler and place over bottom of double boiler. Stir until chocolate is melted.

When patties are chilled, using a dipping fork or dipping spoon, dip patties mixture into the melted chocolate. Place on parchment paper. Set up at room temperature.

Store in a covered container.

Yield: 60 patties

Mint Sandwich

Few can resist creamy mint sandwiched between layers of rich, dark chocolate.

        3/4 pound dark chocolate
        1/2 pound white chocolate
        3 teaspoons vegetable oil
        3 to 5 drops of green color
        1/4 teaspoon peppermint flavoring, or
        1/8 teaspoon peppermint oil

Line a cookie sheet with parchment paper. Set aside.

Separately, chop the white and dark chocolates into 1-inch pieces. Fill the bottoms of two double boilers with very hot tap water. Put the white and dark chocolate into separate top pans and place over bottoms. Add 2 teaspoons of the vegetable oil to the dark chocolate, and the remaining 1 teaspoon of vegetable oil to the white chocolate. Stir until chocolates are melted and oil is incorporated.

To the melted white chocolate, add the green color and peppermint flavoring.

Pour half the melted dark chocolate onto the prepared cookie sheet, and spread it thinly. Try to keep it in an 8- X 10-inch rectangular shape. When the first layer is almost firm, about 15 minutes, spread the green layer on top, keeping the same shape. Again, wait until the green layer is almost firm. Spread the remaining dark chocolate on top until the green layer is covered.

Let the candy layers harden, and cut with a sharp knife which has been dipped in hot water and dried.

Store in plastic wrap.

Yield: 20 2-inch pieces

Raspberry Jellies

Jewel-like raspberry jellies are beautiful as well as delicious.

2 1/2 cups granulated sugar
3 ounces liquid pectin
2 cups cool water
1 1/2 cups light corn syrup
1 10-ounce jar raspberry jam
1 tablespoon liquid citric acid, OR 3/4 teaspoon citric acid
   granules and 1 tablespoon hot water
3 to 4 drops red food coloring
1 cup super fine granulated or confectioners' sugar for rolling

Line an 8-inch square pan with foil and butter the foil generously. Set aside.

If using the citric acid granules, dissolve in the 1 tablespoon hot water. Let stand.

Heat the corn syrup to boiling in a small saucepan or in the microwave.

Place the sugar, pectin and water in a heavy 6-quart saucepan. Slowly add the cool water and stir until smooth. Bring mixture to a boil on medium-high heat, stirring constantly with a wooden spoon. Add the heated corn syrup. Place a candy thermometer into the saucepan and cook rapidly, stirring constantly over medium-high, to 220 degrees.

Add the raspberry jam and red food coloring. Stir and heat to 248 degrees. Remove from the heat and add the citric acid.

Pour into the prepared pan. Set up at room temperature. Cut into 1-inch squares and roll in the super fine or confectioners' sugar.

Wrap each piece in plastic wrap and store in an airtight container.

Yield: 64 pieces

Walnut-Applesauce Jellies

Two favorites, walnuts and applesauce, combine uniquely in this tempting treat. Use your microwave to save time.

    2 1/2 cups granulated sugar
    4 tablespoons unflavored pectin
    2 cups cool water
    1 1/2 cups light corn syrup
    1 15-ounce can applesauce
    1 tablespoon liquid citric acid, OR 3/4 teaspoon citric acid
    granules and 1 tablespoon hot water
    1 cup nuts, such as walnuts
    1 cup super fine granulated sugar or confectioners' sugar

Line an 8-inch square pan with foil and generously butter the foil. Set aside.

If using the citric acid granules, dissolve in the 1 tablespoon hot water. Let stand.

Finely chop nuts; set aside.

Heat the corn syrup to boiling in a small saucepan, or in the microwave.

Place the sugar, pectin and water in a heavy 6-quart saucepan. Slowly add the cool water and stir until smooth. Bring mixture to a boil on medium-high heat, stirring constantly with a wooden spoon. Add the heated corn syrup. Place a candy thermometer into the saucepan and cook rapidly, stirring constantly over medium-high, to 220 degrees.

Add the applesauce. Stir and heat to 248 degrees. Remove from the heat and add the citric acid and the chopped nuts.

Pour into the prepared pan. Set up at room temperature. Cut into 1-inch squares and roll in the super fine or confectioners' sugar.

Wrap each piece in plastic wrap and store in an airtight container.

Yield: 64 pieces

CHILDHOOD
FANTASIES

Cinnamon Candy Apples

Fresh, crisp apples coated with a cinnamon-flavored candy shell are traditional family favorites.

8 to 10 wooden ice cream sticks, about 4 1/2 inches long
8 to 10 red apples, medium size
2 1/2 cups granulated sugar
1 1/4 cups light corn syrup
1 cup water
1/2 teaspoon cinnamon oil
1 teaspoon red food coloring

Wash and dry the apples. Remove the stems and insert the sticks.

Line a cookie sheet with foil and generously butter the foil. Set aside.

Place the sugar, syrup and water in a heavy 4-quart saucepan. Heat over medium-high heat, stirring with a wooden spoon, until sugar is dissolved. Place a candy thermometer into the saucepan and heat to 290 degrees.

Remove from the heat and quickly stir in the color and cinnamon oil. Tilt the pan and quickly dip the apples until well coated. Place the apples on the prepared cookie sheet for candy to harden.

Pour any extra syrup mixture onto the buttered cookie sheet. When hard, break into bite-sized pieces.

Wrap the apples in plastic wrap and secure around the stick if they are not going to be eaten within a few hours.

Yield: 8 to 10 candy apples

Crunchy Malt Balls

"My twin brother and I were very different when it came to eating our favorite candy, malt balls. He liked to crunch his up immediately, while I let mine dissolve slowly on my tongue."

- Sweet Memories

1/2 pound white chocolate
2 cups malted milk powder
1 pound milk chocolate for dipping

Line a cookie sheet with parchment paper; set aside.

Chop the white chocolate into 1-inch squares. Fill the bottom of a double boiler with very hot tap water. Put the chopped white chocolate in the top of the double boiler and place over bottom of double boiler. Stir until chocolate is melted.

Remove from heat, and add the malt powder 1 tablespoon at a time to the melted white chocolate. Stir well after each addition. Add enough powder to be able to form balls, about 1 1/2 cups total.

Using a measuring spoon, drop teaspoon size balls into the remaining malt powder, and roll into round balls. Place on the prepared cookie sheet and allow to set up until firm, approximately 1 hour.

Meanwhile, chop the milk chocolate into 1-inch pieces. Fill the bottom of a double boiler with very hot tap water. Put the chopped chocolate in the top of the double boiler and place over bottom of double boiler. Stir until chocolate is melted.

Using a dipping fork or dipping spoon, dip rolled mixture into the melted chocolate, and return to prepared cookie sheet.

Store in an airtight container.

Yield: 30 pieces

Hard Candy Lollipops

The word "lollipop" probably derives from the colloquial "loll," meaning to dangle the tongue, plus "pop." Whatever the source, everyone agrees lollipops are a delightful adventure for the tongue.

    1 1/4 cups granulated sugar
    1/2 cup light corn syrup
    1/2 cup water
    5-8 drops food coloring
    1-2 teaspoons flavoring (such as cherry, mint, etc.)
    1/8 teaspoon citric acid
    18-20 sucker sticks, 4 - 6-inches long

Generously oil 2 cookie sheets. If using candy molds, wash and dry the molds. Grease the molds with oil and place on an oiled cookie sheet. If using a metal mold, oil, insert stick and clamp closed with metal clip.

Place the sugar, syrup and water in a heavy 3-quart saucepan. Cook over medium heat, stirring with a wooden spoon until sugar is dissolved. Place a candy thermometer into the saucepan and heat to 300 degrees, stirring occasionally. Remove from heat.

Working quickly, stir in the coloring, flavoring and citric acid. As quickly as possible, pour into the molds. If not using molds, pour spoonful size puddles onto the oiled cookie sheet, covering about 1 1/2 inches of the one end of the sucker stick. Cool until hard.

Store wrapped in plastic wrap or cellophane sucker bags.

Yield: 18 to 20 suckers

Marshmallows

Rolled in confectioners' sugar or dipped in chocolate, these fluffy treats are wonderful.

2/3 cup cool water
2 1/2 tablespoons unflavored gelatin
2 1/2 cups sugar
1 cup hot water
1 1/2 cups light corn syrup
1 1/2 teaspoons vanilla
1 cup confectioners' sugar, for rolling

Line an 8-inch square pan with foil, and butter foil generously. Set aside.

Soak the gelatin in 2/3 cup of cool water in a large mixing bowl, ready to beat.

Place the sugar, hot water and corn syrup in a heavy 4-quart saucepan. Cover, and bring to a boil. Remove lid, and place a candy thermometer into the saucepan. Heat to 245 degrees. Remove from heat.

Turn the mixer on medium, and slowly pour hot sugar mixture into the gelatin mixture, mixing constantly. When the mixture begins to thicken, add the vanilla. Beat on medium-high, and continue to increase speed until the marshmallow sticks to the beaters, about 10 minutes.

Pour into the prepared pan. Let cool, about 1 hour.

When cool, pour onto a surface which has been dusted with confectioners' sugar. Cut into 1 1/2-inch squares with wet scissors. Roll in confectioners' sugar, or dip in melted chocolate.

Store in an airtight container.

Yield: 35 marshmallows

Marshmallow Crispies

This light and crunchy sweet snack is easy to prepare and a favorite of children . . . and adults.

    1/2 cup butter
    5 cups mini marshmallows
    7 cups crisp rice cereal

Line a 9 X 13-inch pan with plastic wrap. Set aside.

Melt the butter in a heavy 4-quart saucepan. Add the marshmallows and cook over low heat, stirring with a wooden spoon until marshmallows are melted. Remove from heat and add the cereal. Stir just until blended.

Immediately pour into the prepared pan, and press down with your hand to flatten. Cut into 2-inch squares, or cut into shapes with cookie cutters and decorate with candies or sprinkles.

Yield: 24 squares

Popcorn Balls

"When our family gathered for Christmas, Grandpa, dressed in a Santa suit, gave each child a brightly wrapped popcorn ball from his pack."

- Sweet Memories

5 to 6 quarts of popped popcorn (1 quart equals 2 cups)
1 3/4 cups granulated sugar
1 cup light corn syrup
4 tablespoons butter
1 cup water
1 teaspoon white vinegar
1/2 teaspoon vanilla
1/4 cup butter, for your hands

Pop the popcorn, measure and keep warm in a large, oven-proof bowl in a 225 degree oven.

Place the sugar, corn syrup, butter, water and vinegar in a heavy 4-quart saucepan. Cover, and cook over medium-high heat for 5 minutes. Remove the lid, and place a candy thermometer into the saucepan. Stir with a wooden spoon, and heat to 250 degrees. Remove from heat and add the vanilla.

Slowly pour the syrup mixture over the hot popped corn while stirring it.

When cool enough to handle, butter your hands and form into 3 1/2-inch balls.

Store wrapped individually in plastic wrap.

Yield: 15 popcorn balls

Salt Water Taffy

Before you begin, line up a partner to help pull the taffy. That's half the fun!

2 1/2 cups granulated sugar
2 tablespoons cornstarch
2 teaspoons liquid glycerin
1 cup light corn syrup
1 cup water
1 1/2 teaspoons salt
3 tablespoons butter
1 to 2 teaspoons flavoring, such as cherry, mint, orange, etc.
Food color (optional)

Generously grease a 10- X 15-inch jelly roll pan. Set aside. Lightly oil a heavy 4-quart saucepan.

Mix the sugar and cornstarch together and place into the prepared saucepan. Stir in the glycerin, corn syrup, water and salt. Heat, stirring with a wooden spoon, over medium heat until the sugar is dissolved. Bring to a boil. Cover, and let boil for 3 to 4 minutes. Remove cover, and place a candy thermometer into the saucepan. Heat to 258 degrees. Remove from heat and carefully stir in the butter and flavoring.

Pour into the prepared pan and let cool enough to handle, approximately 10 minutes. Turn the cooling taffy over with a greased metal spatula to speed up the cooling process.

When the taffy is cool enough to handle, butter hands well, and form the taffy into a ball. Begin stretching into ropes. Pull until light in color and texture. The more air you pull into the taffy, the softer it will be. Pulling takes approximately 10 minutes.

With buttered scissors, cut in 1-inch pieces. Wrap in waxed paper squares, and twist the ends of the papers.

Yield: 95 taffy pieces

Creamy Cocoa Taffy

Cocoa taffy is a fine old favorite that never goes out of style.

1 1/4 cups sugar
3/4 cup light corn syrup
1/3 cup cocoa
1/8 teaspoon salt
2 teaspoons white vinegar
1/4 cup evaporated milk
1 tablespoon butter

Butter 9-inch square pan; set aside. In heavy 2-quart saucepan, stir together sugar, corn syrup, cocoa, salt and vinegar.

Cook over medium heat, stirring constantly, until mixture boils. Add evaporated milk and butter. Continue cooking, stirring occasionally. Place a candy thermometer into the saucepan and heat to 248 degrees, stirring occasionally. (Bulb of candy thermometer should not rest on bottom of saucepan.) This is called "firm-ball stage," when syrup dropped into very cold water forms a firm ball which does not flatten when removed from water.

Pour mixture into prepared pan. Cool until lukewarm and comfortable to handle. Butter hands. Immediately stretch taffy, folding and pulling until light in color and hard to pull. The longer the taffy is pulled, the softer it will be.

Place taffy on table; pull into 1/2 inch-wide strips (twist two strips together, if desired). Cut into 1-inch pieces with buttered scissors. Wrap individually.

Store in a covered container.

Yield: About 72 pieces , or 1-1/4 pounds

Oven Caramel Corn

Fill a bag with nutty caramel corn and you're ready for a day at the circus or a romp in the park.

7 to 8 quarts of popped popcorn (1 quart equals 2 cups)
2 cups peanuts (or nuts of your choice)
2 1/2 cups light brown sugar
1 cup and 4 tablespoons butter (2 1/2 sticks)
1 teaspoon salt
3/4 cup light corn syrup
1 teaspoon baking soda
3 teaspoons liquid butter flavoring

Pop the popcorn, measure, and place into a large mixing bowl.

Roast the nuts on an edged cookie sheet in a 325 degree oven for 10 minutes. Remove nuts from oven, and reduce oven heat to 200 degrees.

Butter two edged cookie sheets, or 2 jelly roll pans. Set aside.

Place the sugar, butter, syrup and salt in a heavy 4-quart saucepan. Bring the mixture to a boil, and let boil for 5 minutes.

Remove from heat. Stir in the soda and butter flavoring. Mixture will foam. Pour sugar mixture over the popcorn and mix well. Working quickly, add the roasted nuts and stir again. Spread the mixture out on the two prepared cookie sheets.

Bake in a 200 degree oven for 1 hour. Stir every 15 minutes. Remove from oven and set up at room temperature.

Store in an airtight container.

Yield: 7 to 8 quarts.

Chocolate Pizza

Great to serve for a children's party. Or, with an adult's help making the crispy chocolate "crust," children can decorate their own "pizza" to eat or take home.

    1 pound milk chocolate
    1/2 pound white chocolate
    3 tablespoons butter
    2 cups crisp rice cereal
    4 large green gum drops
    1 cup of your favorite nuts
    Green and red maraschino cherries, well drained
    Black jelly beans, if desired

Chop the chocolates into 1-inch pieces. Fill the bottoms of two double boilers with very hot tap water. Put the white- and milk chocolates in the tops of separate double boilers and place over the bottoms of double boilers. Stir until chocolate is melted.

Sprinkle granulated sugar on the top of the gum drops so they do not stick. With a rolling pin, flatten the gum drops on a sugar-coated cutting board. Roll to 1/8-inch thickness. Cut into 1/2-inch strips, and press ends together to form a circle in the shape of bell peppers.

Add the 3 tablespoons butter to the milk chocolate, stirring to melt. To this, add the crisp rice cereal and stir until cereal is coated. Pour into a 12-inch pizza pan, keeping the mixture about 1/2-inch thick. Sprinkle the nuts over the top. Press the red and green cherries lightly into the chocolate. Place the black jelly beans around (for olives), pressing lightly. Next, press on the gum drop circles (for bell peppers). Last, but not least, dip a fork into the white chocolate and drizzle all over the top (for cheese). Place into the freezer to 5 to 10 minutes, depending upon the size.

When cool, cut with a pizza wheel.

Yield: 1 12-inch pizza, or 4 6-inch pizzas

HOLIDAY
TREATS

Valentine Log

This cherry-nut center confection is the perfect way to say, "I love you"

    4 to 5 cups confectioners' sugar
    1 tablespoon powdered egg white
    2 to 3 tablespoons water
    3 tablespoons cherry preserves
    1 teaspoon cherry flavor (or candy oil to taste)
    1/2 teaspoon citric acid
    1/2 teaspoon vanilla
    1/2 teaspoon liquid butter flavor
    1/2 cup of your favorite nuts

Place half the confectioners' sugar and the remaining ingredients, except the dipping chocolate, in a large mixing bowl. Mix on low until incorporated, then turn on high for 5 minutes.

Turn mixer off, and add the remaining confectioners' sugar. Mix on low until mixture is uniform and smooth. Chill in refrigerator overnight. Meanwhile, prepare Pliable Fudge.

Pliable Fudge

    1 pound white- or dark chocolate
    10 1/2 ounces sweetened condensed milk

Chop the chocolate into 1-inch pieces. Fill the bottom of a double boiler with very hot tap water. Put the chopped chocolate in the top of the double boiler and place over bottom of double boiler. Stir until chocolate is melted.

Remove from heat and stir in the sweetened condensed milk. Allow mixture to set up at room temperature.

continued on following page ☞ ☞ ☞

Valentine Log *(continued)*

When ready to use the pliable fudge, knead a small piece to make it pliable for molding or rolling. This can be put in the microwave on medium for 2 to 3 seconds to start the softening process prior to kneading.

Roll half of the fudge recipe out into a 4 X 8-inch rectangle between parchment or waxed paper. Dust hands with powdered sugar and form the No-Cook Cherry Nut Center into a log to fit into the fudge. Roll the fudge around the cherry center, starting with the long side. Smooth the seam with your fingers. Prepare garnishes.

> 1 cup chopped nuts
> 1/4 cup cherry flavored chips

Melt the cherry chips in a bowl, over second bowl filled with very hot tap water. Pour onto parchment paper, and spread thin. When set but not hard, cut out 1-inch hearts using a cookie cutter. Allow to set up at room temperature. Remove off parchment paper with a thin knife.

Press the log into the chopped nuts, seam-side down, covering the bottom half the log. Decorate the top with the hearts by pressing lightly onto the log.

Wrap log in plastic wrap and refrigerate until ready to eat. Log will be easier to cut at room temperature. Cut into 1/2-inch circles using a sharp knife.

Store in refrigerator, wrapped in plastic wrap.

Yield: 2 logs, 16 slices per log

Fruit and Nut Eggs

Celebrate springtime with chocolate dipped fruit and nut eggs.

    1/3 cup butter
    2 cups sugar
    3/4 cup light corn syrup
    1/2 cup hot water
    7 ounces marshmallow creme
    1 cup confectioners' sugar
    1 1/2 cups candied cherries
    1 cup chopped nuts, such as walnuts
    1 pound milk or dark chocolate for dipping

Line cookie sheet with parchment paper; set aside.

Melt the butter, then allow to cool to room temperature. Coarsely chop the nuts.

Place the sugar, syrup and water in a heavy 3-quart saucepan on medium heat. Place a candy thermometer into the saucepan and heat, stirring constantly, to 265 degrees.

Remove from heat and add the marshmallow creme. Beat until almost firm, by hand or in a mixer. Add the melted butter, confectioners' sugar, candied fruit and chopped nuts. Mix well and chill for 2 to 3 hours, or overnight.

While chilling, chop the chocolate into 1-inch pieces. Fill the bottom of a double boiler with very hot tap water. Put the chopped chocolate in the top of the double boiler and place over bottom of double boiler. Stir until chocolate is melted.

Divide the chilled mixture into 12 pieces and form into egg shapes. Using a dipping fork or dipping spoon, dip eggs into the melted chocolate. Place on prepared cookie sheet.

Store covered in refrigerator.

Yield: 12 eggs

Divinity

This heavenly, soft white candy is appropriately named. It is simply divine!

3 cups granulated sugar
3/4 cup light corn syrup
2/3 cup water
1/4 teaspoon salt
3 egg whites
1 1/2 teaspoons vanilla
1 1/2 cups nuts, such as walnuts

Butter a cookie sheet; set aside.

Place the egg whites in a mixing bowl, and set aside, ready to beat.

Finely chop nuts; set aside.

Place the sugar, corn syrup, water and salt in a heavy 4-quart saucepan. Bring to a boil over medium heat. Cover and heat for 3 minutes. Remove the lid, and place a candy thermometer in the saucepan. When mixture reaches 225 degrees, turn on the mixer and beat the egg whites until stiff, but not dry, as the syrup mixture continues to cook.

When syrup mixture reaches 248 degrees, slowly pour about half the syrup mixture into the beaten egg whites, beating constantly on low. Continue beating slowly while heating the remaining syrup to 270 degrees. Very slowly, pour the remaining syrup into the egg white mixture, mixing constantly on low, until syrup is incorporated.

Increase speed to medium, and beat until mixture loses its gloss and soft peaks form. Mix in the vanilla and nuts.

Drop by teaspoonful onto the prepared cookie sheets. Let set out, uncovered, overnight.

Store in an airtight container.

Yield: 55 pieces

Honey Divinity

"Her divinity was so sweet with honey, I saw an envious bee peeking in the kitchen window."

- Sweet Memories

3 cups granulated sugar
3/4 cup honey
2/3 cup water
1/4 teaspoon salt
3 egg whites
1 1/2 teaspoons vanilla
1 1/2 cups nuts, such as walnuts

Butter a cookie sheet and set aside.

Place the egg whites in a mixing bowl, and set aside, ready to turn on.

Finely chop nuts; set aside.

Place the sugar, honey, water and salt in a heavy 4-quart saucepan. Bring to a boil over medium heat. Cover and heat for 3 minutes. Remove the lid, and place a candy thermometer in the saucepan. When mixture reaches 225 degrees, turn on the mixer and beat the egg whites until stiff, but not dry, as the syrup mixture continues to cook.

When syrup mixture reaches 248 degrees, slowly pour about half the syrup mixture into the beaten egg whites, beating constantly on low. Continue beating slowly while heating the remaining syrup to 270 degrees. Very slowly, pour the remaining syrup into the egg white mixture, mixing constantly on low, until syrup is incorporated.

Increase speed to medium, and beat until mixture loses its gloss and soft peaks form. Mix in the vanilla and nuts.

Drop by teaspoonful onto the prepared cookie sheets. Let set out, uncovered, overnight.

Store in an airtight container.

Yield: 55 pieces

Marzipan

Another name for this confection is "marchpane." By any name, it's a classic.

        1 1/4 cups almond paste
        2 large egg whites
        1/2 teaspoon vanilla
        3-4 cups confectioners' sugar
        1/2 teaspoon rum or almond flavoring
        Paste coloring (available at cake and candy making supply stores)

Place the almond paste in a large mixing bowl and mix on low speed until soft. Add the egg whites and rum, and mix well. Mix in confectioners' sugar, adding a cup or so at a time. Pour mixture on a cutting board dusted with confectioners' sugar and knead in the last cup of the sugar. Marzipan should feel like heavy pie dough.

Knead in paste colors. Mold into the shapes of fruits or vegetables. Use yellow for bananas and pears, orange for carrots and pumpkins, red for strawberries and apples, purple for plums and grapes, green for green beans and leaves. Use white for potatoes, then poke with round toothpick and dust with cocoa powder.

Marzipan can also be rolled into a 3/4-inch ball and dipped in melted chocolate.

Store in an airtight container.

Yield: 40 pieces

Stuffed Dates

"When the days turned cold, I loved to sit in Mama's warm kitchen and help her stuff dates; then I stuffed my little cheeks with them!"

- Sweet Memories

3 ounces cream cheese
1/2 cup butter (do not substitute margarine)
1/8 teaspoon liquid butter flavoring
1/8 teaspoon coconut flavor, or 1/2 teaspoon orange juice
   concentrate
3-3 1/2 cups confectioners' sugar
2 8-ounce packages pitted dates
1/2 cup additional confectioners' sugar for dusting hands
3/4 pound whole almonds or walnuts (optional)

Allow cream cheese and butter to come to room temperature in a large mixing bowl. When softened, thoroughly mix the cream cheese and butter. Add the liquid butter and coconut flavorings. Gradually add the confectioners' sugar, a cup at a time, until the mixture is thick enough to form into a roll.

Dust hands with 1/2 cup additional confectioners' sugar, and break off date-sized pieces. Roll into a ball, and stuff into the dates. If desired, dates can be garnished with nuts.

Store in an airtight container in refrigerator.

Yield: 60 dates

Sugarplum Fairies

These sweet sugarplum fairies will dance in your head and tickle your taste buds.

1 12-ounce package pitted prunes
1 8-ounce package chopped dates
1 small container of candied pineapple
2/3 cup pecans
1/3 cup graham cracker crumbs
3/4 teaspoon grated orange rind
1/4 teaspoon grated lemon rind
3/4 cup super fine sugar
1 1/2 pounds white chocolate for dipping

Finely chop the nuts.

Place the prunes, dates and pineapple in a food processor and chop for one minute, or until finely chopped. Place into a large bowl, and add the pecans, graham cracker crumbs and orange and lemon rinds. Mix well. Cover and chill for 2 hours.

Chop the chocolate into 1-inch pieces. Fill the bottom of a double boiler with very hot tap water. Put the chopped chocolate in the top of the double boiler and place over bottom of double boiler. Stir until chocolate is melted.

Shape fruit mixture into 3/4-inch balls and roll in the super fine sugar. Using a dipping fork or dipping spoon, dip rolled mixture into the melted chocolate, and place on parchment paper.

Store in an airtight container.

Yield: 65 pieces

Christmas Ribbon Fudge

Ribbons of colorful candy fudge add to the glory of the Christmas season.

6 cups confectioners' sugar
1/2 cup melted butter
1 1/2 teaspoons vanilla
5 tablespoons whipping cream
2 ounces dark chocolate
1/2 cup nuts
2-3 drops green food coloring
2-3 drops red food coloring
3 tablespoons maraschino cherries
1/2 cup confectioners' sugar for kneading

Line a 6-inch square pan or 1 metal ice cube tray with plastic wrap and set aside. Sift the confectioners' sugar. Chop the nuts finely. Chop and drain the cherries. Chop the chocolate into 1-inch pieces. Fill the bottom of a double boiler with very hot tap water. Put the chopped chocolate in the top of the double boiler and place over bottom of double boiler. Stir until chocolate is melted.

Place 5 3/4 cups of the sugar, melted butter and vanilla in a large mixing bowl. Mix slowly on low until incorporated. Add enough of the whipping cream to make the mixture hold the form of a ball. Place onto a cutting board which has been dusted with confectioners' sugar and knead until smooth. Divide into thirds.

To one third, add the melted chocolate and mix well. To another third, add the green color and the nuts. Mix well. To the remaining third, add the red color, chopped cherries and the remaining 1/4 cup of the sifted confectioners' sugar, and mix well.

Place the chocolate mixture into the prepared pan. Spread and pat to level. Place the cherry layer on the top and pat to level. Lastly, place the green layer on top, and pat to level. Chill in the refrigerator for 2 to 3 hours. Remove from pan and cut into 1/2 X 2-inch ribbons.

Store in an airtight container in refrigerator.

Yield: 35 pieces

Candy Canes

"Every year when we were young, my brother and I made candy canes to hang on the Christmas tree. They didn't stay there long, however, for little by little they disappeared into our tummies."

— Sweet Memories

2 1/2 cups granulated sugar
3/4 cup light corn syrup
1/2 cup water
1/2 teaspoon cream of tartar
2 teaspoons peppermint flavoring, or 1 teaspoon peppermint oil
1 teaspoon red food coloring
1 teaspoon white food coloring, optional (available at cake or candy
    supply stores)
4 tablespoons butter, for your hands
Oil for counter

Generously oil two 12- X 16-inch cookie sheets; set aside. Lightly oil a heavy 3-quart saucepan.

Place the sugar, syrup, water and cream of tartar into the prepared saucepan. Stir with a wooden spoon, and cook over medium high heat until sugar is dissolved. Continue to cook, without stirring. Place a candy thermometer into the saucepan and heat to 270 degrees.

Remove from heat and stir in flavoring. Pour half of the mixture into another saucepan. Add the red food coloring to one of the mixtures, and if using white, add to the second mixture; mix well. Pour each separately onto the oiled cookie sheets. Allow to cool 10 to 15 minutes.

Oil a flat counter top. When cool enough to handle, butter you hands and work with 1/8 of the mixture at a time. Pull and roll each portion by hand into 1/2-inch wide lengths. Lay a length of white and one of red side by side. Twist one end and the other end the opposite way at the same time until lengths are fully twisted. Cut into 8-inch lengths with oiled scissors and form into canes. Place on a lightly buttered cookie sheet to completely harden.

Store wrapped in plastic wrap or in a cellophane candy bag.

Yield: 25 canes

Christmas Fruit Nut Wreath

Varying shapes and colors make this a beautiful and unique holiday gift or centerpiece.

    1 pound milk chocolate
    1 pound dark chocolate
    1 cup crisp rice cereal
    1/2 pound roasted cashews
    1/2 pound roasted pecans
    1/2 pound Brazil nuts
    1/2 pound Filbert nuts
    1 small container each candied red and green cherries
    1 small container candied pineapple

Chop the milk- and dark chocolates into 1-inch pieces. Fill the bottoms of two double boilers with very hot tap water. Put each of the chopped chocolates in separate double boiler tops and place over bottoms. Stir until chocolates are melted.

Pour half of the milk chocolate into a bowl and mix in the rice cereal. Spray an 8-inch ring mold lightly with non-stick spray. Pour mixture into mold and place in the freezer for 5 to 8 minutes, or until set. Remove by tapping gently upside down on the counter top. Allow ring to come to room temperature.

Dip the nuts and fruit into the dark chocolate and remaining milk chocolate. Instead of immersing every nut or fruit in the melted chocolate, dip only some of the nuts and fruit. This will allow the shapes and colors to be seen. Immediately after dipping, place them on the ring. The melted chocolate will act as glue. Cover the entire rounded part of the wreath. The different shapes and colors make this a beautiful and unique gift or centerpiece. A bow can be added to the top or bottom of the wreath for a finishing touch.

Store wrapped in plastic wrap.

Yield: 1 wreath

Truffle Tree

This impressive tree of sweet delights will linger long in the holiday memories of family and friends.

      1 1/2 pounds white chocolate
      3 tablespoons butter
      1/3 cup heavy cream
      1/4 cup half and half
      1 teaspoon vanilla
      1 pound white chocolate for dipping

Chop the 1 1/2 pounds white chocolate into 1-inch pieces. Fill the bottom of a double boiler with very hot tap water. Put the chopped chocolate in the top of the double boiler and place over bottom of double boiler. Stir until chocolate is melted.

Scald the cream and half and half by placing in a medium saucepan over medium heat, and bring just to the boiling point. Do not allow mixture to boil. Let cool to lukewarm. Add the scalded creams and the vanilla to the melted chocolate and mix until well blended and smooth.

Chill mixture in the refrigerator, stirring every 5 to 10 minutes until set up. Dust your hands with confectioners sugar. Make twenty five 1-inch balls, and ten 3/4-inch balls. Refrigerate 8 to 10 minutes.

Meanwhile, chop the 1 pound of white chocolate into 1-inch pieces. Fill the bottom of a double boiler with very hot tap water. Put the chopped chocolate in the top of the double boiler and place over bottom of double boiler. Stir until chocolate is melted. Using a dipping fork or dipping spoon, dip rolled mixture into the melted chocolate, and place on parchment paper. Set up at room temperature. Meanwhile, prepare Chocolate Truffles as follows.

continued on following page ☞ ☞ ☞

Truffle Tree *(continued)*

Chocolate Truffles

> 3/4 cup (1 1/2 sticks) butter
> 3/4 cup cocoa
> 1 can (14 ounces) sweetened condensed milk
> 1 tablespoon vanilla extract
> 1 pound dark chocolate for dipping

In heavy saucepan over low heat, melt butter. Add cocoa; stir until smooth. Add sweetened condensed milk; cook and stir constantly until mixture is thick, smooth and glossy, about 4 minutes.

Remove from heat; stir in vanilla. Cover and refrigerate 3 to 4 hours or until firm. Shape into twenty five 1-inch balls, and ten 3/4-inch balls. Refrigerate until firm, 8 to 10 minutes.

Meanwhile, chop the 1 pound of dark chocolate into 1-inch pieces. Fill the bottom of a double boiler with very hot tap water. Put the chopped chocolate in the top of the double boiler and place over bottom of double boiler. Stir until chocolate is melted. Using a dipping fork or dipping spoon, dip rolled mixture into the melted chocolate, and place on parchment paper. Set up at room temperature. Prepare Chocolate Leaves.

Chocolate Leaves

> 35 leaves (Any edible or non-poisonous leaf can be used. Rose or
>   lemon leaves work well because they have nice veins.)
> 3/4 pound milk chocolate
> 1 tablespoon vegetable oil

Chop the chocolate into 1-inch pieces. Fill the bottom of a double boiler with very hot tap water. Put the chopped chocolate in the top of the double boiler and place over bottom of double boiler. Stir until chocolate is melted. Add the vegetable oil. This will prevent the chocolate from setting up hard, and will make it easier to remove from the leaves.

continued on following page ☞ ☞ ☞

Truffle Tree *(continued)*

Wash the leaves you are going to use, and pat dry. Using a small soft pastry or painting brush, paint the chocolate on the back of the leaf where the veins are heavier. For easier removal, two coats of chocolate may be used.

Set up at room temperature. When set, gently run your thumb between the leaf and chocolate to separate, starting at the wide end of the leaf.

Now begin assembly of the tree:

> 1/2 pound white chocolate
> 1/2 pound dark chocolate
> 1/2 pound milk chocolate
> 1 — 4- X 12-inch styrofoam cone
> 50 toothpicks, cut in half
> Waxed paper
> 1 pedestal cake plate

Melt the white-, dark- and milk chocolates separately as described above. Cover the cone with waxed paper. Use some of the melted chocolate to glue the paper to the cone. Trim the top and bottom if necessary so the waxed paper is even with the cone. Use more melted chocolate to glue the cone to the center of the cake plate.

Using a dipping fork, drizzle some of the melted white chocolate over the chocolate truffles, and some of the dark chocolate over the white truffles. Allow to set up at room temperature.

Starting at the bottom of the cone, press 1/2 of the toothpick into the cone at a 45 degree angle, about 1 inch from the bottom. Gently press one of the larger truffles onto the toothpick. Alternate dark and light truffles as you move up the cone. Once three-quarters of the way up the cone, switch to the smaller truffles. Dip the stem end of the chocolate leaves into the melted milk chocolate and quickly stick them in between the truffles to cover any of the cone which is visible.

Yield: 1 tree with approximately 70 truffles

Crystallized Violets

Candied violets (and other candied edible flowers) add a unique decorator touch to cakes and frozen or gourmet desserts. You can buy them or, with a little practice, make your own. Prepare them during the spring season when violets are blooming, and store them to use all year.

    36 violets
    1 egg white
    1 cup super-fine sugar
    10 drops violet flavor (recipe follows)

Buy or pick 36 violets. Be sure they have not been sprayed with pesticide. Remove the stems, leaving only the flower. Wash carefully with water and dry with a tissue.

Beat the egg white until foamy, not stiff.

Line a cookie sheet with parchment paper. Generously sprinkle the super fine sugar on the parchment paper. Set aside.

Gently brush the egg whites onto both sides of the flower with a small, flat, soft 1/4-inch brush. Then, using a small strainer filled with remaining super-fine sugar, carefully coat the flower with sugar. Use a toothpick to help manipulate the flowers, keeping the petals open. Place the flowers on the prepared cookie sheet, stem-side down. Let them dry at room temperature, uncovered, for 2 to 3 days.

If desired, violet flavor can be added to the egg white before beating. Violet flavor can be made by simmering washed violets in 1 cup of water for 15 to 20 minutes. Let cool and strain.

These will keep almost forever stored in an airtight container in a cool place.

Yield: 36 violets

Candy Leaves

Any edible or non-poisonous leaf can be used to create candy leaves. Rose and lemon leaves work well because they have nice veins.

3/4 pound milk or dark chocolate
1 tablespoon vegetable oil

Chop the chocolate into 1-inch pieces. Fill the bottom of a double boiler with very hot tap water. Put the chopped chocolate in the top of the double boiler and place over bottom of double boiler. Stir until chocolate is melted. Add the vegetable oil. This will prevent the chocolate from setting up and will make it easier to remove from the leaves.

Wash the leaves you are going to use, and pat dry. Using a small soft pastry or painting brush, paint the chocolate on the back of the leaf where the veins are heavier. For easier removal, two coats of chocolate may be used.

Set up at room temperature. When set, gently run your thumb between the leaf and chocolate to separate, starting at the wide end of the leaf. Use to decorate cakes, pies, mousse and much more.

Store, covered, at room temperature.

Yield: 35 to 50 leaves

Candied Orange or Grapefruit Rind

Candied fruit rind prepared during the holidays can be stored easily and enjoyed throughout the year.

Rind from 5 oranges or 2 grapefruits

Cut the peels into sixths by running a knife from top to bottom. Using your fingers, remove the sections of peel and pull out the membrane and most of the soft white inner rind. Cut the rind into 1/8-inch wide strips. Prepare syrup as follows.

    2 tablespoons salt
    1/2 cup water
    2 1/2 cups granulated sugar
    3/4 cup additional granulated sugar

Place the prepared rinds into a heavy 3-quart saucepan. Add salt and enough water to cover three inches above rinds. Bring to a boil and simmer gently for 10 minutes. Drain well. Cover again with water and simmer an additional 10 minutes. Drain well. Cover with water a third time, and simmer 10 minutes more. Drain well.

Add 1/2 cup fresh water and 2 1/2 cups sugar to the rinds and bring to a boil. Reduce heat and simmer until syrup is absorbed and the rinds look translucent.

Roll rinds in 1/2 cup of the additional granulated sugar. Spread remaining 1/4 cup sugar onto a parchment-lined cookie sheet. Place rinds on prepared cookie sheet. Preheat oven to 250 degrees. Turn oven off and place the rinds in the oven. Let stay overnight in oven to dry.

Store indefinitely in an airtight container.

Tuxedo Berries

These berries are dressy enough for New Year's Eve or any elegant party.

50 2-inch strawberries
1 pound dark chocolate
1/2 pound white chocolate
5 teaspoons vegetable oil
1 small cake decorating bag or small plastic bag

Line two cookie sheets with parchment paper. Set aside. Wash and dry the berries and place in the refrigerator to chill.

Chop the white- and dark chocolates into 1-inch pieces. Fill the bottoms of two double boilers with very hot tap water. Put the chopped chocolates in the tops of the separate double boilers and place over bottoms of double boilers. Add 3 teaspoons of the oil to the dark chocolate and 2 teaspoons of the oil to the white chocolate. Stir until chocolates are melted and oil is incorporated.

Dip the front of the berry in the white chocolate, from the point to the top of the berry, leaving about 1/2 inch from the top of the berry uncovered. Place on the parchment paper, berry side down, and set up at room temperature.

Next, dip the berries in the dark chocolate, at an angle, from the bottom point up one side, then up the other. Roll from the front side to the back, a little higher than the white chocolate. This will leave a white triangle "V", with the wide end at the top of the berry (to look like the front of a man's shirt and coat). Place back on the parchment paper, white insert up, to set up again at room temperature.

Place about 1/4 cup of the melted dark chocolate in a small parchment or plastic bag. Cut a very small hole off the end. To make buttons, place 3 small dots in the center of the white, and make a sideways figure "8" shape for a bow tie above the buttons. A real show stopper!

Use the same day.

Store covered in refrigerator. Berries should be eaten within 24 hours.

Yield: 50 berries

TRUFFLES

Chocolate Truffles I

A sweet-and-simple truffle recipe.

      3/4 cup (1 1/2 sticks) butter
      3/4 cup cocoa
      1 can (14 ounces) sweetened condensed milk
      1 tablespoon vanilla extract
      Cocoa or powdered sugar

In a heavy saucepan over low heat, melt butter. Add cocoa; stir until smooth. Add sweetened condensed milk; cook and stir constantly until mixture is thick, smooth and glossy, about 4 minutes.

Remove from heat; stir in vanilla.

Cover and refrigerate 3 to 4 hours or until firm. Shape into 1 1/4-inch balls. Roll in cocoa or powdered sugar. Or, if desired, roll balls in chopped nuts. Refrigerate until firm, 1 to 2 hours.

Store covered in refrigerator.

Yield: About 2 1/2 dozen candies

Chocolate Truffles II

Chocolate dipped truffles are as fun to make as they are to eat.

1 1/2 pounds dark chocolate
4 tablespoons butter
3/4 cup heavy cream
1 pound dark chocolate for dipping
1/2 cup cocoa powder for dusting hands

Line a cookie sheet with parchment paper; set aside.

Chop the 1 1/2 pounds dark chocolate into 1-inch pieces. Fill the bottom of a double boiler with very hot tap water. Put the chopped chocolate and the butter in the top of the double boiler and place over bottom of double boiler. Stir until chocolate is melted and butter is incorporated.

Scald the cream by placing in a medium saucepan over medium heat, and bring just to the boiling point. Do not allow cream to boil. Then let cool to 100 degrees. Stir the cooled cream into the chocolate mixture until well blended. Allow the mixture to cool at room temperature, or chill in the refrigerator, stirring every 5 to 10 minutes.

While mixture is chilling, chop the remaining 1 pound dark chocolate into 1-inch pieces. Fill the bottom of a double boiler with very hot tap water. Put the chopped chocolate in the top of the double boiler and place over bottom of double boiler. Stir until chocolate is melted.

Dust hands with the cocoa powder and roll chilled mixture into 3/4-inch balls. Place on the prepared cookie sheet, and chill for 8 to 10 minutes. Using a dipping fork or dipping spoon, dip rolled mixture into the melted chocolate, and return to prepared cookie sheet.

Store covered in refrigerator.

Yield: 50 truffles

Chocolate Espresso Truffles

Kahlua or espresso coffee add drama to these dark chocolate truffles.

1 pound dark chocolate
3 tablespoons butter
2/3 cup whipping cream
1 egg yolk
1/3 cup Kahlua, or 2 tablespoons espresso coffee
1/2 cup cocoa powder, for dusting hands
1 pound dark or bittersweet chocolate for dipping

Line a cookie sheet with parchment paper; set aside.

Chop the 1 pound of dark chocolate into 1-inch pieces. Fill the bottom of a double boiler with very hot tap water. Put the chopped chocolate in the top of the double boiler and place over bottom of double boiler. Stir until chocolate is melted.

While the chocolate is melting, scald the cream by placing in a medium saucepan over medium heat, and bring just to the boiling point. Do not allow cream to boil. Cool the cream to lukewarm.

Whisk the egg yolk and kahlua into the cooled cream. Add the cream mixture to the melted dark chocolate. Stir well. Chill 2 to 3 hours.

While the cream mixture is chilling, chop the dark or bittersweet chocolate into 1-inch pieces. Fill the bottom of a double boiler with very hot tap water. Put the chopped chocolate in the top of the double boiler and place over bottom of double boiler. Stir until chocolate is melted.

When the cream mixture is set, dust your hands with cocoa powder and roll mixture into 3/4-inch balls. Place on the prepared cookie sheet and chill in the refrigerator for 8 to 10 minutes. Using a dipping fork or dipping spoon, dip rolled mixture into the melted chocolate, and place back on the prepared cookie sheet to set up.

Store covered in refrigerator.

Yield: 50 truffles

Chocolate Mint Truffle

Choose mint liqueur or peppermint oil for this sweet treat.

      3/4 pound milk chocolate
      3 tablespoons butter
      1/2 cup whipping cream
      2 egg yolks
      1 tablespoon mint liqueur, or 1/8 teaspoon peppermint oil
      1/2 cup cocoa powder, for dusting hands
      1 pound milk or dark chocolate for dipping

Line a cookie sheet with parchment paper and set aside.

Chop the 3/4 pound milk chocolate into 1-inch pieces. Fill the bottom of a double boiler with very hot tap water. Put the chopped chocolate in the top of the double boiler and place over bottom of double boiler. Stir until chocolate is melted.

While chocolate is melting, scald the cream by placing in a medium saucepan over medium heat, and bring just to the boiling point. Do not boil. Allow cream to cool to lukewarm. Whisk the egg yolks and mint liqueur into the lukewarm cream. Add the cream mixture to the melted chocolate, stirring well. Chill for 2 to 3 hours.

When the chocolate mixture is chilled, dust hands with cocoa powder and roll mixture into 3/4-inch balls. Place on prepared cookie sheet and chill for 8 to 10 minutes.

Meanwhile, chop the 1 pound of milk- or dark chocolate into 1-inch pieces. Fill the bottom of a double boiler with very hot tap water. Put the chopped chocolate in the top of the double boiler and place over bottom of double boiler. Stir until chocolate is melted. Using a dipping fork or dipping spoon, dip rolled mixture into the melted chocolate, and place back on prepared cookie sheet to set up.

Store covered in refrigerator.

Yield: 35 truffles

Espresso Truffles

Espresso truffles are perfect gifts for friends who are coffee enthusiasts.

    3/4 cup (1 1/2 sticks) butter
    3/4 cup cocoa
    1 can (14 ounces) sweetened condensed milk
    1 teaspoon vanilla extract
    1 1/4 teaspoons powdered instant espresso or instant coffee
    Cocoa

In heavy saucepan over low heat, melt butter. Add cocoa; stir until smooth. Add sweetened condensed milk; cook and stir constantly until mixture is thick, smooth and glossy, about 4 minutes.

Remove from heat; stir in vanilla and espresso or coffee.

Cover and refrigerate 3 to 4 hours or until firm. Shape into 1 1/4-inch balls. Roll in cocoa. Or, if desired, roll balls in chopped nuts. Refrigerate until firm, 1 to 2 hours.

Store covered in refrigerator.

Yield: About 2 1/2 dozen truffles

Hawaiian Truffles

At your next luau, serve this regally rich Hawaiian-style confection.

    1 cup shredded coconut
    1 cup macadamia nuts
    1/2 cup heavy cream
    1/2 cup coconut cream (available in cans in liquor departments)
    1 pound white chocolate
    1 egg yolk
    2 teaspoons dark rum
    1 pound dark chocolate for dipping

Line a cookie sheet with parchment paper; set aside.

Toast the coconut and macadamia nuts on additional two cookie sheets, in a 325 degree oven until lightly brown, about 5 minutes. When cool, finely chop the nuts. Set aside.

Chop the white chocolate into 1-inch pieces. Fill the bottom of a double boiler with very hot tap water. Put the chopped white chocolate in the top of the double boiler and place over bottom of double boiler. Stir until chocolate is melted.

While white chocolate is melting, heat the heavy cream and coconut cream in a separate saucepan. When cream mixture boils, remove from heat and let cool for 5 minutes. Whisk the egg yolk into the cooled cream. Add cream mixture to the melted white chocolate. Next, add the rum and roasted coconut. Cover with plastic wrap and chill until thick, stirring occasionally.

Meanwhile, chop the dark chocolate into 1-inch pieces. Fill the bottom of a double boiler with very hot tap water. Put the chopped chocolate in the top of the double boiler and place over bottom of double boiler. Stir until chocolate is melted.

continued on following page ☞ ☞ ☞

Hawaiian Truffles *(continued)*

When white chocolate mixture is set, dust your hands with confectioners' sugar and roll chilled mixture into 3/4-inch balls. Place on prepared cookie sheet. Chill 8 to 10 minutes.

Using a dipping fork or dipping spoon, dip rolled mixture into the melted dark chocolate, and roll in the finely chopped macadamia nuts. Set up at room temperature on parchment paper.

Store covered in refrigerator.

Yield: 50 truffles

Hazelnut Truffles

I like these truffles dipped in chocolate and topped with a fresh hazelnut.

    45 shelled hazelnuts
    1 pound milk or dark chocolate
    3 tablespoons butter
    2/3 cup whipping cream
    4 tablespoons hazelnut- or chocolate-flavored liqueur
    1/2 cup cocoa powder

Chop the chocolate into 1-inch pieces. Fill the bottom of a double boiler with very hot tap water. Put the chopped chocolate in the top of the double boiler and place over bottom of double boiler. Stir until chocolate is melted.

Place the hazelnuts in a 9 X 13-inch pan, and roast them in a 325 degree oven until golden brown, approximately 8 to 10 minutes. Let cool at room temperature. If you want to remove the skins, rub gently with a towel while still warm.

Scald the cream by placing in a medium saucepan over medium heat, and bring just to the boiling point. Do not allow cream to boil. Let cream cool to lukewarm. Add the cooled cream and liqueur to the chocolate mixture; mix well. Chill for 2 to 3 hours, or until firm.

Dust hands with some of the cocoa powder and roll chilled mixture into 1-inch balls. Roll the truffle in the remaining cocoa powder to coat well. Press a roasted hazelnut into the top so that half the nut still shows.

These could also be dipped in melted chocolate and topped with a nut.

Store covered in refrigerator.

Yield: 36 truffles

Nut Truffles

Roll nut truffles in cocoa or powdered sugar for added richness.

> 3/4 cup (1 1/2 sticks) butter
> 3/4 cup cocoa
> 1 can (14 ounces) sweetened condensed milk
> 1 tablespoon vanilla extract
> 3/4 cup coarsely chopped toasted pecans
> Cocoa or powdered sugar

To toast pecans, heat oven to 350 degrees. Spread pecan halves in single layer in an ungreased shallow baking pan. Bake for 5 to 7 minutes, stirring occasionally. Cool before chopping.

In heavy saucepan over low heat, melt butter. Add cocoa; stir until smooth. Add sweetened condensed milk; cook and stir constantly until mixture is thick, smooth and glossy, about 4 minutes.

Remove from heat; stir in vanilla and pecans.

Cover and refrigerate 3 to 4 hours or until firm. Shape into 1 1/4-inch balls. Roll in cocoa or powdered sugar. Refrigerate until firm, 1 to 2 hours.

Store covered in refrigerator.

Yield: About 2 1/2 dozen truffles

Orange Truffles

Those who adore truffles report these are perfect with early morning orange juice or coffee.

> 1 pound milk- or dark chocolate
> 2 tablespoons super-fine sugar
> 3 tablespoons butter
> 2/3 cup whipping cream
> 1 1/2 tablespoons orange liqueur
> 2 teaspoons finely grated orange rind
> 1 egg yolk
> 1/2 cup cocoa powder, for dusting hands
> 1 pound dark chocolate for dipping

Line a cookie sheet with parchment paper; set aside.

Chop the 1 pound milk- or dark chocolate into 1-inch pieces. Fill the bottom of a double boiler with very hot tap water. Put the chopped chocolate, sugar, butter and cream in the top of the double boiler and place over bottom of double boiler. Stir until chocolate is melted and mixture is smooth. Remove top of double boiler from the bottom, and let mixture cool to lukewarm.

In a small bowl, whisk the egg yolk into the liqueur. Add liqueur mixture and grated rind to the lukewarm chocolate. Stir and mix together. Let cool in the refrigerator for 2 to 3 hours, or until set.

Meanwhile, chop the remaining dark chocolate into 1-inch pieces. Fill the bottom of a double boiler with very hot tap water. Put the chopped chocolate in the top of the double boiler and place over bottom of double boiler. Stir until chocolate is melted.

Dust your hands with cocoa powder. Roll chilled mixture into 1-inch balls. Place on prepared cookie sheet and refrigerate for 8 to 10 minutes. Using a dipping fork or dipping spoon, dip rolled mixture into the melted chocolate, and place back on parchment paper. Set up at room temperature.

Store covered in refrigerator.

Yield: 50 truffles

Rum Nut Truffles

For a unique taste sensation try this blend of rum, pecans, and cocoa.

    3/4 cup (1 1/2 sticks) butter
    3/4 cup cocoa
    1 can (14 ounces) sweetened condensed milk
    1 teaspoon vanilla extract
    2 tablespoons rum, or 1 teaspoon rum extract
    3/4 cup coarsely chopped toasted pecans
    Cocoa or powdered sugar

To toast pecans, heat oven to 350 degrees. Spread pecan halves in single layer in an ungreased shallow baking pan. Bake for 5 to 7 minutes, stirring occasionally. Cool before chopping.

In heavy saucepan over low heat, melt butter. Add cocoa; stir until smooth. Add sweetened condensed milk; cook and stir constantly until mixture is thick, smooth and glossy, about 4 minutes.

Remove from heat; stir in vanilla, rum or rum extract, and pecans.

Cover and refrigerate 3 to 4 hours or until firm. Shape into 1 1/4-inch balls. Roll in cocoa or powdered sugar. Refrigerate until firm, 1 to 2 hours.

Store covered in refrigerator.

Yield: About 2 1/2 dozen truffles

Turtle Truffles

These are the richest, and perhaps the most delicious, of all turtle confections.

3/4 cup butter
2 cups brown sugar, firmly packed
Pinch of salt
3/4 cup light corn syrup
1 14-ounce can sweetened condensed milk
1/2 teaspoon vanilla
3 tablespoons heavy whipping cream
1 1/4 cups pecans
12 ounces milk chocolate
4 tablespoons butter
1/3 cup caramel ice cream topping
1/2 cup cocoa powder
1 1/2 pounds milk chocolate for dipping

Line a 9-inch square pan with foil and butter it generously. Set aside.

In a heavy 4-quart saucepan, melt the 3/4 cup butter over medium heat. Using a wooden spoon, stir in brown sugar, salt and corn syrup until dissolved. Then, add the sweetened condensed milk. Place a candy thermometer into the saucepan and, stirring constantly, heat to 243 degrees.

Remove from heat. Stir in vanilla. Pour into prepared pan. Allow to set up overnight at room temperature. When set, cut into squares.

Meanwhile, line a cookie sheet with parchment paper; set aside.

Chop the pecans finely; set aside.

Chop the chocolate into 1-inch pieces; set aside.

continued on following page ☞ ☞ ☞

Turtle Truffles *(continued)*

Scald the cream by placing in a medium saucepan over medium heat and bring just to the boiling point. Do not allow cream to boil. Cool cream to lukewarm.

Fill the bottom of a double boiler with very hot tap water. Put the 12 ounces of chopped chocolate in the top of the double boiler and place over bottom of double boiler. Stir until chocolate is melted. Beat in the caramel ice cream topping and cooled cream. Chill for 2 to 3 hours, or until firm.

While truffle mixture is chilling, melt the dipping chocolate as described above.

Roll the cooled caramel into 1/4 teaspoon size balls, and place on a cookie sheet lined with parchment paper.

Dust hands with cocoa powder and roll the chilled truffle mixture into 3/4-inch balls. Wrap the truffle ball around the small ball of caramel. Return to the cookie sheet and chill for 8 to 10 minutes. Using a dipping fork or dipping spoon, dip truffle into the melted chocolate, and roll in the finely chopped pecans and place back on parchment paper. Allow to set up at room temperature.

Store covered in refrigerator.

Yield: 72 turtles

White Chocolate Truffles

White chocolate centers dipped in more white chocolate are simply heavenly!

1 1/2 pounds white chocolate
3 tablespoons butter
1/3 cup heavy cream
1/4 cup half and half
1 teaspoon vanilla
1 pound white chocolate for dipping

Chop the 1 1/2 pounds white chocolate into 1-inch pieces. Fill the bottom of a double boiler with very hot tap water. Put the chopped chocolate in the top of the double boiler and place over bottom of double boiler. Stir until chocolate is melted.

Scald the cream and half and half by placing in a medium saucepan over medium heat, and bring just to the boiling point. Do not allow mixture to boil. Let cool to lukewarm. Add the scalded creams and the vanilla to the melted chocolate and mix until well blended and smooth.

Chill mixture in the refrigerator, stirring every 5 to 10 minutes until set up. Dust your hands with confectioners' sugar and roll chilled mixture into 3/4-inch balls. Refrigerate 8 to 10 minutes.

Meanwhile, chop the 1 pound of white chocolate into 1-inch pieces. Fill the bottom of a double boiler with very hot tap water. Put the chopped chocolate in the top of the double boiler and place over bottom of double boiler. Stir until chocolate is melted.

Using a dipping fork or dipping spoon, dip rolled mixture into the melted chocolate, and place on parchment paper. Set up at room temperature.

Store covered in the refrigerator.

Yield: 55 truffles

Whipped Cream Truffles

Use a pastry bag and tiny candy cups to make these melt-in-your mouth delights. You can store them in the refrigerator for up to a month, or freeze them for two to three months.

1 pound milk or dark chocolate
4 tablespoons butter
3/4 cup heavy cream
1/2 teaspoon flavoring, such as rum or crème de menthe
40 petit four cups, or small candy cups

Before you begin, place a large mixing bowl in the freezer to chill.

Chop the chocolate into 1-inch pieces. Fill the bottom of a double boiler with very hot tap water. Put the chopped chocolate and butter in the top of the double boiler and place over bottom of double boiler. Stir until chocolate is melted and butter is incorporated.

Scald the cream by placing in a medium saucepan over medium heat, and bring just to the boiling point. Do not allow cream to boil. Let cream cool to 100 degrees.

Pour the cooled cream into the chocolate mixture and stir. Allow to set up at room temperature, or chill in the refrigerator, stirring every 5 to 10 minutes.

When set, whip the mixture in the chilled bowl until fluffy. Mixture should hold a peak.

Spoon mixture into a 12- or 14-inch pastry bag with a #4 French Star tip. Pipe the mixture into individual petit four cups. Chill as soon as possible, as they melt easily at room temperature.

Cover and store in the refrigerator for up to 1 month, or freeze for 2 to 3 months.

Yield: 40 truffles

White Sour Cream Truffles

The secret to this recipe's flavor success is the subtle tang of sour cream.

3/4 pound white chocolate
2 tablespoons butter
1/2 cup sour cream
1 teaspoon rum (optional)
1 pound white chocolate for dipping

Line a cookie sheet with parchment paper; set aside.

Chop the 3/4 pound white chocolate into 1-inch pieces. Fill the bottom of a double boiler with very hot tap water. Put the chopped white chocolate in the top of the double boiler and place over bottom of double boiler. Stir until white chocolate is melted. Cool to lukewarm, approximately 10 minutes.

To this lukewarm chocolate, add the sour cream and rum, and beat until blended and smooth. Chill in the refrigerator for 1 to 2 hours, or until firm, stirring every 5 to 10 minutes.

Dust hands with confectioners' sugar, and roll mixture into 3/4-inch balls. Place on prepared cookie sheet. Chill 8 to 10 minutes.

Meanwhile, chop the 1 pound of white chocolate into 1-inch pieces. Fill the bottom of a double boiler with very hot tap water. Put the chopped white chocolate in the top of the double boiler and place over bottom of double boiler. Stir until white chocolate is melted. Using a dipping fork or dipping spoon, dip rolled mixture into the melted chocolate, and place back on cookie sheet to set up at room temperature.

Store covered in refrigerator.

Yield: 30 truffles

Nancy Shipman's Story

"She's sugar and spice and everything nice."

Nancy Shipman proudly claims three "home states" — Oklahoma, Arkansas, and California. Her family was from Poteau, Oklahoma, but Nancy was born in Fort Smith, Arkansas, which happened to have the hospital closest to her family's home. When she was a young child, her father accepted a management position in Southern California, where Nancy grew up.

Nancy can't recall a time when she wasn't busy having fun in the kitchen. As a pre-schooler, she enjoyed "helping" prepare family meals, and with the encouragement and guidance of her mother, Nancy learned to cook and bake by the time she started school. Her childhood was enriched by culinary experiences. As a young adult, Nancy learned new and exciting skills, and she developed a special fondness for creating elegant cakes and candies.

Eventually, Nancy's fancy became a career. While working in a party supply store in La Habra, Nancy was given the opportunity to create a cake-decorating and candy-making department. Soon, she began teaching classes in cake decorating and simplified methods of candy making. Customers and students returned again and again, appreciative of Nancy's knowledge, excellent teaching skills and bubbly enthusiasm. Nancy had found her niche.

In 1982, Nancy moved to Northern California and, in partnership with her husband, Dave, and cheered on by family and friends, opened Nancy's Fancy's in Santa Rosa. The warm and friendly business has grown rapidly and currently offers an extensive variety of classes (and videotapes) on candy-making, cake decorating, and creating other specialty items; supplies for cake decorating, candy-making, and general baking; supplies for holidays, parties and weddings; and much more. Customers, who soon count themselves as friends, are many and loyal.

For Nancy Shipman, life is one sweet success after another.

Nancy's Classes on Videotape

Beginner Candy
Candy-making as easy as 1, 2, 3 using candy molds.
Running time 30 minutes
$19.95

Terrific Truffles
How to make terrific truffles and a truffle tree centerpiece.
Running time 30 minutes.
$19.95

Beginner Cakes
Introduction to and decorating party cakes.
Running time 50 minutes.
$19.95

Wedding Cakes
How to decorate, assemble and transport wedding cakes.
Running time 30 minutes.
$19.95

Panorama Eggs
How to mold, assemble and decorate sugar Easter eggs.
Running time 30 minutes.
$19.95

Gingerbread House
How to cut, bake and assemble a delightful gingerbread house.
Running time 90 minutes.
$24.95

To order Nancy Shipman's classes on videotapes, call or write:

Nancy's Fancy's
3480 Airway Drive
Santa Rosa, CA 95403
707-546-2253

Nancy's Fancy's Store Supplies

CANDY

Guittards
Real white chocolate
Real milk chocolate
Real dark chocolate
Real bittersweet chocolate

Merckens Rainbow Coating
Butterscotch
Cocoa, light
Cocoa, dark
Green
Green, dark
Orange
Pink
Peanut butter
Red
White
Yellow

Guittards Melt'n Mold Coating
Chocolate, dark
Chocolate, light
Chocolate, milk
Light green - peppermint
Pink - strawberry
White - vanilla
Yellow - lemon

Candy Fillings
Caramel loaf - vanilla,
    ready to use
Vanilla - easy butter
    cream
Wilton cherry
Wilton chocolate

OTHER INGREDIENTS

Candy oils
Amaretto
Anise
Apricot
Banana
Black walnut
Bordeaux
Bubble gum
Butterscotch
Chocolate
Cinnamon
Cream de menthe
Concord grape
Irish cream
Kahlua coffee
Lemon
Macadamia nut
Maple
Orange
Peppermint
Piña colada
Pineapple
Praline & cream
Raspberry
Red hot cinnamon
Root beer
Rum butter
Sour green apple
Spearmint
Strawberry
Vanilla
Watermelon
Wild cherry
Wintergreen

Caster sugar - super fine sugar

Citric acid

Desiccated coconut - macaroon

Drivert sugar

Egg albumen

Fondant sugar

Glucose

Invertase

Lecithin

Nulomoline - invert sugar

Oil-based candy colors
Black
Blue
Green
Orange
Pink
Red
Violet
Yellow

Paramount crystals

Powder candy colors
Black
Blue
Brown
Burgundy
Green

continued on following page ☞ ☞

Powder candy colors
(continued)

Gold
Orange
Pink
Red
Royal
White
Yellow

Raw nuts
Almonds
Cashews
Peanuts
Pecans
Macadamia

Candy boxes and bags
Boxes, white: 1/4 lb., 1/2 lb., 1 lb., 1-1/2 lb., 2 lb., 3 lb.
Boxes, with windows: 1 lb., 1 pc; 1/2 lb., 2 pc; 1 lb., 2 pc.
Seasonal boxes: Valentine, Easter, Halloween, Christmas.
Truffle box: 1 pc.
Clear cellophane bags: 1/4 lb., 1/2 lb., 1 lb.

Candy molds, plastic
For chocolate candy
For hard candy

EQUIPMENT

Candy brushes:
#1 (flat 1/4"),
#4 (flat 1/2")

Candy funnel

Candy pads

Candy oil dropper

Candy thermometer

Cookie sheet

Dipping forks

Elastic metallic ties:
#1/2 and #1 boxes

Fluted paper candy cups:
#4sp brown, #5a colors and prints, #8 colors

Foil squares:
3"x3"- gold with cherries

Foil squares:
4"x 4"- blue, fuchsia, green, gold, red, royal, pink, purple

Marble slab

Pans:
8" x 8", 9" x 9", 9" x 13"

Parchment paper

Plastic squeeze bottles

Rubber spatula

Waxed caramel papers

Sucker sticks:
Assorted sizes

To order Nancy Shipman's candy-making supplies, call or write:

Nancy's Fancy's
3480 Airway Drive
Santa Rosa, CA 95403
707-546-2253

INDEX

A

Acetic acid, definition and use, 10
Almond Bark, 62
Almond Clusters, 82
Almond paste, definition and use, 10
Apricot Chews, 89

B

Baking soda, definition and use, 10
Bark, almond, 62
Bark, crunchy lemon, 63
Bark, marbled, 64
Berries, tuxedo, 162
Bloom, on chocolate, 15
Bon Bons, coconut, 111
Bordeaux, 100
Brown and White Balls, 106
Brown sugar, definition and use, 10
Butter Mints, 123
Butterscotch Chews, 88
Butterscotch Creams, 101
Buttery Cashew Brittle, 59
Brittles and Barks
    Almond Bark, 62
    Buttery Cashew Brittle, 59
    Coconut Mixed Nut Brittle, 58
    Crunchy Lemon Bark, 63
    English Toffee, 61
    Macadamia Nut Brittle, 60
    Marbled Bark, 64
    Peanut Brittle, 57
Butterscotch Fudge, 45
Butterscotch Fudge Cut-Outs, 39

C

Candied Orange or
    Grapefruit Rind, 161
Candy Apples, 133
Candy Canes, 154
Candy coloring, definition and use, 10, 25
Candy Hash, 91
Candy Leaves, 160
Candy-making supplies, 8, 10, 182
Candy molds, care and use, 19, 20, 21, 22, 23, 24
Candy painting, 25
Caramel-Coconut Roll Ups, 69
Caramel Corn, 141
Caramels and Nougats
    Caramel-Coconut Roll Ups, 69
    Chocolate Caramels, 67
    Chocolate Nougat, 72
    Cream Nut Caramels, 68
    Honey Nut Nougats, 73
    Nougat Caramel Pinwheels, 74
    Peanut Nougat Log, 76
    Time Saving Caramels, 70
    Vanilla Nougat, 71
Cashew Crunch, 90
Caster sugar, definition and use, 10
Cherry-Nut Centers, no-cook, 116
Cherry-Nut Log, 145
Childhood Fantasies
    Cinnamon Candy Apples, 133
    Chocolate Pizza, 142
    Creamy Cocoa Taffy, 140
    Crunchy Malt Balls, 134
    Hard Candy Lollipops, 135

Childhood Fantasies *(continued)*
    Marshmallows, 136
    Marshmallow Crispies, 137
    Oven Caramel Corn, 141
    Popcorn Balls, 138
    Salt Water Taffy, 139
Chocolate
    Baking chocolate, 15
    Definition and use of, 10, 14, 15,
    Dietetic chocolate, 15
    Milk chocolate, 15
    Real chocolate, 10, 14, 15, 16
    Sweet- and semi-sweet chocolate, 15
    Tempering, 15, 16
    White chocolate, 15
Chocolate Almond Fudge, 50
Chocolate Caramels, 67
Chocolate Cherry Yummies, 48
Chocolate Espresso Truffles, 167
Chocolate Fudge, 47
Chocolate Malted Creams, 105
Chocolate Mint Patties, 124
Chocolate Mint Truffles, 168
Chocolate Truffles I, 165
Chocolate Truffles II, 166
Chocolate Nougat, 72
Chocolate Pizza, 142
Christmas Fruit Nut Wreath, 155
Christmas Ribbon Fudge, 153
Cinnamon Candy Apples, 133
Cinnamon Coffee Squares, 107
Citric acid, definition and use, 10
Coconut oil, definition and use, 10
Confectioners' coating, definition
    and use, 11, 15
Confectioners' ginger, definition, 11
Confectioners' sugar, definition
    and use, 11
Corn syrup, definition and use, 11
Cream, which type to use, 11

Cream Centers
    Bordeaux, 100
    Brown and White Balls, 106
    Butterscotch Creams, 101
    Chocolate Malted Creams, 105
    Cinnamon Coffee Squares, 107
    Creamy Chocolate Centers, 102
    Lemon Creams, 103
    Maple Creams, 98
    Maple Nut Creams, 99
    Mix and Match Butter Cream
        Centers, 97
    No-Cook Vanilla Butter Cream
        Center, 95
    Orange Cream Center, 104
    Quick and Easy Cream Center, 96
Colorings, see *candy colors*
Cream Cheese Mints, 125
Cream Nut Caramels, 68
Creamy Chocolate Centers, 102
Creamy Cocoa Taffy, 140
Creamy Double Decker Fudge, 42
Cocoa fudge, 29, 30, 31
Coconut, raw chip type, definition
    and use, 12
Coconut Bon Bons, 111
Coconut Candy Bar Center, 112
Coconut Kisses, 113
Coconut Mixed Nut Brittle, 58
Coffee squares, cinnamon, 107
Crunchy Date Nut Balls, 114
Crunchy Lemon Bark, 63
Crunchy Malt Balls, 134
Crunchy Peanut Butter Centers, 118
Crystallized Violets, p. 159

D

Dates, stuffed, 151

Desiccated (macaroon) coconut,
    definition and use, 11
Dipping and coating, how to, 18
Divinity, 148
Double Decker Fudge, 42, 49
Drivert sugar, definition and use, 11
Dry corn syrup, definition and use, 11
Dry egg white, definition and use, 11
Dry fondant, definition and use, 11
Double Decker Fudge, 49

E

Easter Egg, fruit and nut, 147
Easy Rocky Road, 33
Egg albumen, see *dry egg white*, 11
Egg, fruit and nut, 147
English Toffee, 61
Equipment and Supplies, 8
Espresso Truffles, 169

F

Fairies, sugarplum, 152
Filled molded candy, 20
Flat molds, 20
Foolproof Chocolate Fudge, 46
Foolproof Dark Chocolate Fudge, 34
Foolproof Fudge Cut-Outs, 40
Full solid, full hollow, and filled
    hollow molding, 21
Frappé, definition, 11
Fruit and Nut Center, 115
Fruit and Nut Centers
    Coconut Bon Bons, 111
    Coconut Candy Bar Center, 112
    Coconut Kisses, 113
    Crunchy Date Nut Balls, 114
    Crunchy Peanut Butter Centers, 118
    Fruit and Nut Center, 115

No-Cook Cherry Nut Centers, 116
    Peanut Butter Balls, 117
Fruit and Nut Eggs, 147

Fudge
    Butterscotch Fudge, 45
    Butterscotch Fudge Cut-outs, 39
    Chocolate Almond Fudge, 50
    Chocolate Cherry Yummies, 48
    Chocolate Fudge, 47
    Christmas Ribbon Fudge, 153
    Creamy Double Decker Fudge, 42
    Double Decker Fudge, 49
    Easy Rocky Road, 33
    Foolproof Chocolate Fudge, 46
    Foolproof Dark Chocolate Fudge, 34
    Foolproof Fudge Cut-Outs, 40
    Golden Maple Fudge, 37
    Layered Mint Chocolate Fudge, 41
    Marshmallow-Nut Cocoa Fudge, 31
    Melt-In-Your-Mouth Fudge, 32
    Nutty Rich Cocoa Fudge, 30
    Peanut Butter Fudge Cut-Outs, 38
    Penuche, 54
    Pliable Fudge #1, 52
    Pliable Fudge #2, 53
    Peanut Butter Fudge I, 43
    Peanut Butter Fudge II, 44
    Rich Cocoa Fudge, 29
    Rocky Road Fudge, 35
    Touchdown Chocolate Fudge, 34
    Ultra Semi-Sweet Fudge
        Cut-Outs, 51
    White Fudge, 36

G

Glazed Nuts, 81
Glucose, definition and use, 12
Golden Maple Fudge, 37

H

Hard Candy Lollipops, 135
Hash, candy, 91
Hawaiian Truffles, 170
Hazelnut Truffles, 172
Holiday Treats
   Candied Orange or Grapefruit
     Rind, 161
   Candy Canes, 154
   Candy Leaves, 160
   Christmas Fruit Nut Wreath, 155
   Christmas Ribbon Fudge, 153
   Crystallized Violets, p. 159
   Divinity, 148
   Fruit and Nut Eggs, 147
   Honey Divinity, 149
   Marzipan, 150
   Stuffed Dates, 151
   Sugarplum Fairies, 152
   Truffle Tree, 156
   Tuxedo Berries, 162
   Valentine Log, 145
Honey, which to use, 12
Honey Divinity, 149

I

Invert sugar, definition and use, 12
Invertase, definition and use, 12

J

Jellies, raspberry, 129
Jellies, walnut-applesauce, 130

K

Kisses, coconut, 113

L

Layered Mint Chocolate Fudge, 41
Leaves, candy, 160
Lecithin, definition and use, 12
Lemon Bark, 63
Lemon Creams, 103
Log, Valentine cherry nut, 145
Lollipops, 135

M

Macadamia Nut Brittle, 60
Macadamia Nut Clusters, 83
Malt Balls, 134
Maple Creams, 98
Maple Fudge, 37
Maple Nut Creams, 99
Marble slab, description and use, 9
Marbled Bark, 64
Marchpane, see *marzipan*, 150
Marshmallow Crispies, 137
Marshmallow-Nut Cocoa Fudge, 31
Marshmallows, 136
Marzipan, 150
Melt-in-Your-Mouth Mints, 126
Melt-In-Your-Mouth Fudge, 32
Mint Chocolate Fudge, layered, 41
Mints and Jellies
   Butter Mints, 123
   Chocolate Mint Patties, 124
   Cream Cheese Mints, 125
   Melt-in-Your-Mouth Mints, 126
   Mint Sandwich, 128
   Peppermint Patties, 127
   Raspberry Jellies, 129
   Walnut-Applesauce Jellies, 130
Mint Sandwich, 128
Mix and Match Butter Cream
   Centers, 97

Molasses, definition and use, 12
Molds/molding candy, see *candy molds*

N

No-Cook Cherry Nut Centers, 116
No-Cook Vanilla Butter Cream
   Center, 95
Non-dairy creamer, when to use, 12
Nougat, chocolate, 72
Nougat, honey nut, 73
Nougat, caramel pinwheels, 74
Nougat, peanut log, 76
Nougat, vanilla, 71
Nulomoline, definition, 12
Nut Truffles, 173
Nuts, Clusters and Chews
   Almond Clusters, 82
   Butterscotch Chews, 88
   Candy Hash, 91
   Cashew Crunch, 90
   Glazed Nuts, 81
   Macadamia Nut Clusters, 83
   Peanut Clusters, 84
   Pralines, 92
   Raisin Clusters, 85
   Tangy Apricot Chews, 89
   Turtles, 86
Nutty Rich Cocoa Fudge, 30

O

Oils and flavorings, definition and
   use, 12
Orange Cream Center, 104
Orange Truffles, 174
Oven Caramel Corn, 141

P

Painting candy with summer
   coating, 25
Paramount crystals, definition
   and use, 12
Peanut Brittle, 57
Peanut Butter Fudge Cut-Outs, 38
Penuche, 54
Peppermint Patties, 127
Pizza, chocolate, 142
Pliable Fudge #1, 52
Pliable Fudge #2, 53
Peanut Butter Balls, 117
Peanut Butter Fudge I, 43
Peanut Butter Fudge II, 44
Peanut Clusters, 84
Popcorn Balls, 138
Pralines, 92

Q

Quick and Easy Cream Center, 96

R

Raisin Clusters, 85
Raspberry Jellies, 129
Raw chip coconut, definition
   and use, 12
Reconstituted egg white, see
   dry egg white, 11
Ribbon fudge, 153
Rich Cocoa Fudge, 29
Rind, candied orange and
   grapefruit, 161
Rocky Road Fudge, 33, 35

Rolling pin, type, 8
Royal icing/frosting, definition
  and use, 13
Rum Nut Truffles, 175

S

Salt Water Taffy, 139
Solid molded candy, 20
Stuffed Dates, 151
Suckers, how to make, 24
Sugarplum Fairies, 152
Summer coating/summer chocolate,
  definition and use, 13, 14, 18
Supplies, candy-making, 8, 10, 182

T

Taffy, cocoa, 139
Taffy, salt water, 139
Tangy Apricot Chews, 89
Tempering chocolate, how to and
  importance of 14, 15, 16, 18
Thermometer, type, importance of and
  how to check for accuracy, 8,
  14, 16
Toffee, English, 61
Touchdown Chocolate Fudge, 34
Truffle Tree, 156
Truffles
  Chocolate Espresso Truffles, 167
  Chocolate Mint Truffles, 168
  Chocolate Truffles I, 165
  Chocolate Truffles II, 166
  Espresso Truffles, 169

  Hawaiian Truffles, 170
  Hazelnut Truffles, 172
  Nut Truffles, 173
  Orange Truffles, 174
  Rum Nut Truffles, 175
  Turtle Truffles, 176
  Whipped Cream Truffles, 179
  White Chocolate Truffles, 178
  White Sour Cream Truffles, 180
Turtle Truffles, 176
Turtles, 86
Tuxedo Berries, 162

U

Ultra Semi-Sweet Fudge Cut-Outs, 51

V

Valentine Log, 145
Vanilla butter cream center, no-cook,
  95
Videotapes, Nancy Shipman's classes,
  181
Violets, crystallized, 159

W

Walnut-Applesauce Jellies, 130
Whipped Cream Truffles, 179
White Chocolate Truffles, 178
White Fudge, 36
White Sour Cream Truffles, 180
Wreath, Christmas fruit and nut, 155

Truffle Tree, *directions page 156*

❏ *Nancy's Candy Cookbook, How to make candy at home the easy way* by Nancy Shipman
softcover, $14.95, 1996 pub.

CHILDREN'S BOOKS & MUSIC

❏ *The Perfect Orange, A tale from Ethiopia* by Frank P. Araujo, PhD; illustrated by Xiao Jun Li
hardcover, $16.95, 1994 pub., Toucan Tales volume 2
(**PBS** *Storytime* **Selection, Fall 1996**; Recommended by *School Library Journal, Faces, MultiCultural Review, Small Press Magazine, The Five Owls, Wilson Library Bulletin*)

❏ *Nekane, the Lamiña & the Bear, A tale of the Basque Pyrenees*
by Frank P. Araujo, PhD; illustrated by Xiao Jun Li   hardcover, $16.95, 1993 pub., Toucan Tales volume 1
(Recommended by *School Library Journal, Publishers Weekly, Kirkus Reviews, Booklist, Wilson Library Bulletin, The Basque Studies Program Newsletter: University of Nevada, BCCB, The Five Owls*)

❏ *The Laughing River, A folktale for peace* by Elizabeth Haze Vega; illustrated by Ashley Smith, 1995 pub.
hardcover book, $16.95 ♡ companion musical audiotape, $9.95 ♡ book & musical audiotape combo, $23.95
(Recommended by *School Library Journal*)

❏ *When Molly Was in the Hospital, A book for brothers and sisters of hospitalized children*
by Debbie Duncan; illustrated by Nina Ollikainen, MD   hardcover, $12.95, 1994 pub.
(**Winner of 1995 Benjamin Franklin Award: Best Children's Picture Book**. Recommended by *Children's Book Insider, School Library Journal, Disabilities Resources Monthly*)

❏ *Night Sounds* by Lois G. Grambling; illustrated by Randall F. Ray
1996 pub., hardcover, $12.95   softcover, $6.95

❏ *Los Sonidos de la Noche* by Lois G. Grambling; illustrated by Randall F. Ray
(Spanish edition of *Night Sounds*), 1996 pub., hardcover, $12.95   softcover, $6.95

❏ *Link Across America, A story of the historic Lincoln Highway* by Mary Elizabeth Anderson
hardcover, $14.95, Spring 1997 pub.

BUSINESS & CAREER

❏ *The Independent Medical Transcriptionist, 2nd edition. The comprehensive guidebook for career success in a home-based medical transcription business* by Donna Avila-Weil, CMT Mary Glaccum, CMT
softcover, $32.95, 1994 pub. (Recommended by *Journal of the American Association for Medical Transcription, Entrepreneur, Small Business Opportunities*)

❏ *Smart Tax Write-offs, Hundreds of tax deduction ideas for home-based businesses, independent contractors, all entrepreneurs* by Norm Ray, CPA   softcover, $12.95, 1996 pub.

❏ *Easy Financials for Your Home-based Business, The friendly guide for busy home entrepreneurs*
by Norm Ray, CPA   softcover, $19.95, 1992 pub.
(Recommended by *Wilson Library Bulletin, The Business Journal, National Home Business Report*)

HISTORY & GENERAL

❏ *20 Tales of California, A rare collection of western stories*, by Hector Lee   softcover, $9.95, 1996 pub.

❏ *Windsor, The birth of a city* by Gabriel A. Fraire   hardcover, $21.95, 1991 pub.

Payment: Check ◇ **Cash** ◇ **Visa** ◇ **MasterCard** ◇ **Discover** ◇ **AMEX**

Card #	Exp date	Signature	
Name			Amount
Address			Phone
City State Zip			Date